Peter Harbison

# Pre-Christian IRELAND

## From the First Settlers to the Early Celts

WITH 139 ILLUSTRATIONS

*Drawings by Edelgard Soergel-Harbison*

THAMES AND HUDSON

THIS IS NUMBER ONE HUNDRED AND FOUR IN THE SERIES
*Ancient Peoples and Places*
FOUNDING EDITOR: GLYN DANIEL

*For my three children, John, Maurice and Ronan*

*Half-title page* Detail of a spiral from the passage-tomb of
Newgrange, Co. Meath.

*Title page* The stone Tanderagee Idol, which perhaps represents
a pagan deity, now on Cathedral Hill, Armagh.

© 1988 Thames and Hudson Ltd, London

First paperback edition with revisions 1994

British Library Cataloguing-in-Publication Data
A catalogue record for this book is available from the British Library

ISBN 0-500-27809-1

Printed and bound in Slovenia by Mladinska Knjiga

# Contents

1 Map of Ireland, with modern counties and place-names mentioned in the text.

# Preface to the Paperback Edition

SOME OF THE SIGNIFICANT changes in our understanding of Ireland's prehistory that have taken place since this book first appeared are selectively summarized below in the form of a bibliographical up-date (for full titles, see Select Bibliography, p.196). One important development is the series of Groningen radiocarbon datings (Brindley, Lanting and Mook, *Journal of Irish Archaeology*, Vols IV–VI, 1987–92), given in calibrated years BP (before the present). These datings indicate the presence of non-megalithic burials, including those of Linkardstown type (p.85), in the southern half of Ireland from 4800 BP onwards, with the earliest of the three periods of use at Poulawack (p.86) dating to around 4485 BP. Portal-tombs (pp.52–56) and court cairns (pp.47–52) emerge some time beforehand in the Early Neolithic, around 5000 BP. The series also suggests that the construction of wedge-tombs (pp.100–2) and *fulachta fian* (pp.110–12) may have started early in the Bronze Age, around 3800 BP, while stone circles (pp.94–98) are now seen as belonging to the later Bronze Age. Further Neolithic houses (pp.32–38) have come to light at Tankardstown, Co. Limerick and Newtown, Co. Meath (Gowen, *Archaeology Ireland* 1 (1), 1987, 6 and 6 (2), 1992, 25 respectively), and evidence of pre-tomb habitation has been unearthed at Knowth (pp.66ff.). The Bronze Age is now being filled out with some simple pottery types hitherto dated to the Neolithic (Woodman, *Antiquity* 66, 1992, 295), and the earliest settlement evidence at Dún Aenghus (p.186) is now attributed to the Late Bronze Age (Cotter, *Archaeology Ireland* 8 (1), 1994, 24). Research has shown that the torc in fig.116 was not found at Clonmacnois, but in Co. Roscommon (Ireland, *PRIA* 92 C, 1992, 123). References to swords of Ballintober type (pp.133 and 148) should read 'swords of Eogan's Class 4' (compare G. Eogan *Catalogue of Irish Bronze Swords*, Dublin 1965, with P.C. Woodman, 'Reviews', *Antiquity* 62, 1988, 810).

E. Shee Twohig's *Irish Megalithic Tombs* (Princes Risborough 1990) succinctly summarizes current knowledge, and J. Waddell's *The Bronze Age Burials of Ireland* (Galway 1990) covers the grave practices of the period. The finds from court cairns have been studied by Herity (*PRIA* 87 C, 1987, 103), while *fulachta fian* are looked at in *Burnt Offerings* (ed. V. Buckley, Dublin 1990). J.P. Mallory and T.E. McNeill's *The Archaeology of Ulster* (Belfast 1991) provides a very good overview of that province's prehistory, including details of recent work at Lyles Hill and Donegore in Co. Antrim (p.37), to which Hartwell's research at Ballynahatty, Co. Down (*Archaeology Ireland* 5 (4), 1991, 12) should be added (p.98). For the Iron Age, the reader should now turn to B. Raftery's *Pagan Celtic Ireland: The Enigma of the Irish Iron Age* (London and New York 1994).

# 1·Introduction

ALTHOUGH IRELAND may have been one of the last countries in Europe to have been colonized by human populations, it is an island which is particularly rich in prehistoric remains. Its anthology of megalithic tombs comes next in number after France and Scandinavia, and, in the Boyne Valley, it has monuments to rival the glory of Mycenae. The rich gold jewellery, unequalled in Western Europe, makes one feel that the country's Bronze Age is a misnomer, and that it should be called its Golden Age. Or, perhaps better, the first of its Golden Ages – the second one being dealt with in Máire and Liam de Paor's *Early Christian Ireland*, which may be regarded as the sequel to this volume in the Ancient Peoples and Places series. The Iron Age in Ireland has much to offer the historian of Celtic art, and the great fort of Dún Aenghus on the Aran Islands must surely be regarded as one of the most magnificent barbaric monuments to be found anywhere in Western Europe.

It is the archaeology of Ireland's prehistoric period, up to the coming of Christianity, which forms the subject of this book. In it, an attempt will be made to summarize the present state of research, taking into account the most recent findings and discoveries. It would not have been possible to write this book without the dedicated work of fellow archaeologists, alive and dead, who may be thanked here one and all for the contributions which they have made to the study of prehistoric Ireland. Prehistory is not just what prehistoric people made of it, but also what archaeologists have made of it today, and this is the reason why the text of this book makes a point of naming the archaeologists who have made the significant contributions. Thirty years ago, Professor Daniel A. Binchy, the well-known Celtic scholar, spoke of 'the imaginative and conflicting speculations of archaeologists, and devotees of that curious science which calls itself prehistory'. Because prehistory – by its very nature – has to deal with speculations, it is natural that the views of archaeologists will conflict, and it is only by weighing up the pros and cons that one can come to the most probable solution to any problem in prehistory, where the absence of writing makes it difficult to make the mute stones speak. Professor Binchy may not have been too far wrong when he called archaeology a 'curious science', yet it certainly is one which becomes not only more interesting, but also more exact, with every passing day. This can be instanced by the revolution caused by the discovery of the radiocarbon dating method, and its even more recent and precise counterpart, dendrochronology, or the science of tree-ring dating.

1

The radiocarbon method attempts to give the date of an organic object by estimating the amount of Carbon 14 which still survives in it, based on the presumption that the carbon content decreases at a steady rate after the death of the object itself. Such radiocarbon dates are purposely preceded by the letter *c.*, for *circa*, as they are only approximate to within a few hundred years of the given date.* But work both in America and Europe on the number of annual rings contained in tree-trunks which have also been radiocarbon dated, has shown that radiocarbon years do not correspond to actual calendar years, the radiocarbon years often being hundreds of years too young. In order to distinguish radiocarbon years from the actual calendar years before or after the birth of Christ (given in capitals as BC or AD), the radiocarbon dates quoted here are followed by the same two letters, but printed in lower case, thus – bc or ad. As an example, one may quote the case of the great passage-tomb at Newgrange which provided a radiocarbon date of *c.*2500 bc, but which is likely to have been built about 600 years earlier, around 3100 BC. In order to provide the true date in calendar years, all the radiocarbon dates given in this book ought to be 'calibrated'. The reason why this calibration has not been carried out automatically throughout the text here is that it has not yet proved possible to calibrate all the radiocarbon years accurately on a sliding scale.

The work of Michael Baillie and his colleagues in the Belfast Conservation Laboratory in providing an accurate tree-ring chronology for the Irish oak back to the year 5289 BC has supplied us now with a major breakthrough, and even though the method may be costly, it is hoped that it will not be long before we will have a reliable guide to the actual difference between radiocarbon and calendar years on the basis of the Belfast tree-ring datings. It ought to be pointed out here, however, that the Belfast laboratory has shown that radiocarbon dates falling between 800 and 400 bc can no longer be relied upon, as they cannot be distinguished from one another, and that they ought to be abandoned therefore.

## The history of research

The early Irish Christians were consumed by a curiosity to find out about what happened in their country before the dawn of history and so, in the eleventh and twelfth centuries, an effort was made in the so-called *Book of Invasions* to reconstruct the relative succession of the series of peoples who were considered to have invaded the country in prehistoric times. But despite the strength of oral tradition in Ireland, the work of the

---

* The varying range of time before or after the given date in which the correct radiocarbon year of the object is likely to fall, commonly known as the standard deviation (for example, 2000 bc plus or minus 100, thus giving a probable date between 2100 and 1900 bc), is omitted here, but it – and the name of the dating laboratory – can normally be obtained by reference to the journal *Radiocarbon*. The Council for British Archaeology's *Site Index to Radiocarbon Dates for Britain and Ireland* of 1971, and its supplements, also give useful summaries.

synthesizing historians who composed the Book need not be taken too literally, for the events they purported to describe are alleged to have taken place 1,000 years or more before they were written down. Furthermore, it was contemporary political reasons which led diligent chroniclers to compile genealogies for ruling families in order to trace their noble ancestry back as far as possible – even to the extent of tracing the line back to Adam and Eve! But, for all their efforts, we can place no reliance on any documentary evidence which tells of happenings or people earlier than the fifth century AD, and it is, therefore, left to the interpretation of the archaeological record to tease out the story of Ireland before St Patrick's christianizing mission.

It is doubtless more than a mere coincidence that it is from the time of the synthesizing historians that we have what may be described as the first Irish archaeological report, in the form of an entry in the old Irish *Annals of Loch Cé*, telling of the finding of an outsize axe and spearhead in the river Galway in the year 1191. For the fact that such a discovery was recorded at all may be a reflection of that same historical curiosity which led to the compilation of the *Book of Invasions*, and which inspired Gaelic kings of the twelfth century to commission religious shrines of metal and to erect High Crosses of stone which would help to recreate the glorious Christian past of three or four centuries earlier. The same fervour can be seen at a lower social level during the 1680s, when the re-erection of fallen crosses epitomized the hopes of the people that the Duke of York, when he would ascend the throne of England as James II, would usher in a period of greater religious freedom and tolerance in Ireland, reminiscent of that which had reigned in centuries past.

Not until 1699, however, when the Welsh antiquary Edward Lhuyd paid his initial visit to Ireland, did we have our first record in more recent times of a real interest in Ireland's prehistoric antiquities. Lhuyd, who was a Keeper at the Ashmolean Museum in Oxford, provided us with the first written account of Newgrange, which had been accidentally opened earlier in the same year. Notices of the discovery of prehistoric objects were recorded spasmodically during the course of the eighteenth century, both by individuals and learned societies, but real progress was not made until the nationalistic sentiments which took Europe by storm in the first half of the nineteenth century awakened among the Irish people a new pride in their country's past. It was during the 1830s that George Petrie, John O'Donovan and Eugene O'Curry, young men with old heads on their shoulders, went out into the field, and in working for the first set of detailed Ordnance Survey six-inch-to-the-mile maps of Ireland, came across and recorded for the first time a vast number of Irish antiquities. Financial cutbacks allowed for the publication of only a single parish-volume of the survey, that of Templemore, which included the plan and account of the Grianán of Aileach (p. 186), then in Co. Derry and now in Co. Donegal.

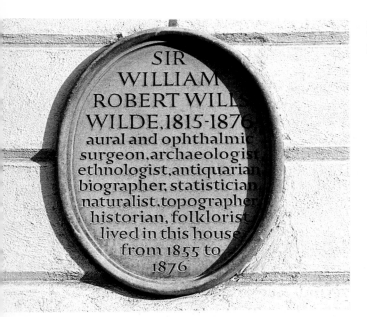

2 Plaque commemorating Sir
William Wilde on the wall of his
house at 1 Merrion Square, Dublin.

SIR
WILLIAM
ROBERT WILDE
WILDE, 1815-1876
aural and ophthalmic
surgeon, archaeologist
ethnologist, antiquarian
biographer, statistician
naturalist, topographer
historian, folklorist
lived in this house
from 1855 to
1876

The reproduction of the typed-up versions of the Ordnance Survey
Letters in the 1920s and 1930s showed us that the work of that noble band
of warriors almost a century earlier had come none too soon, for in many
cases theirs was the only detailed description and illustration of
monuments which have, in the meantime, fallen prey to the claws of the
mechanical digger, and are now not even a heap of rubble in the corner of
some long-neglected field. In his travels, Petrie amassed a collection of
some 1,500 smaller portable antiquities which – like the Iron Age crown
(p. 179) which bears his name – have now passed into the national
collections by way of the Royal Irish Academy, and his endeavours have
earned for him the honorary title of 'Father of Irish Archaeology'. He
ought to share this distinction, however, with Sir William Wilde, surely
one of the most remarkable polymaths ever to grace the Irish scene. His
wide interests are proclaimed on a plaque let into the wall of his residence
2     at No. 1, Merrion Square, Dublin. He fathered not only the genial Oscar,
but also a splendidly detailed three-volume catalogue of the Royal Irish
Academy's extensive collection of antiquities (1857–1862) which must
surely stand, along with Ludwig Lindenschmidt's catalogue of the
Hohenzollern collection at Sigmaringen, as one of the great, if isolated,
highpoints of solid Victorian archaeological cataloguing.

An effort to see the stone and bronze items of the Academy's collection
in a somewhat broader context was undertaken by John Evans, in his
books on stone and bronze implements, of 1897 and 1881 respectively,
which covered Britain as well. Incidentally, his son Arthur, of Knossos
fame, was to play an important role in the history of the Iron Age
Broighter hoard (p. 176). In 1882 Sir John Lubbock's new Monuments

Act became law, but the Church Disestablishment Act of 1869 had already given state protection to Irish monuments for the first time, and this has since been greatly expanded by the Office of Public Works, facilitated by the National Monuments Act of 1930, and its 1954 and 1987 amendments. By 1890, the National Museum had come into being in Dublin, the archaeological material in its displays coming from the Royal Irish Academy's collection, and ten years later George Coffey was named Curator of Irish Antiquities, an important post which has ever since continued to be occupied by a succession of distinguished Keepers. Frank Mitchell thinks that it is not too much to claim that Coffey 'was one of the makers of modern European archaeology', and support for this contention comes from Coffey's famous volumes on *Newgrange* (1912) and *The Bronze Age in Ireland* (1913) which, despite having been written after he had suffered a series of strokes, still remain valuable today. In producing them, Coffey was helped by his successor, E.C.R. Armstrong, who not only updated Wilde's catalogue of gold ornaments, but also gave us the first synthesizing studies on the so-called Hallstatt and La Tène periods in Ireland (pp. 148 and 161).

Excavation in nineteenth-century Ireland was a haphazard affair, scarcely worthy of the modern scientific name. An enormous shaft was dug into the centre of the great tumulus at Dowth in the Boyne Valley, in an unsuccessful attempt to discover a chamber similar to that known from the centre of the neighbouring mound at Newgrange, and other megaliths, too, sadly came in for their share of despoliation. Unfortunately, even reputable names such as that of R.A.S. Macalister, Professor of Archaeology in Dublin, and the great botanist Robert Lloyd Praeger, continued the trend in our own century at Carrowkeel in Co. Sligo (p. 61). There had been a few brighter spots, such as Coffey's excavation of Topped Mountain in Co. Fermanagh in 1897, but it was not until the advent of the Harvard Archaeological Mission – which carried out the first large-scale scientific series of excavations in Ireland in 1932 and subsequent years – that excavation blossomed out to become the science it is now. Under its programme, Hallam L. Movius carefully excavated and published the Mesolithic site at Curran Point, near Larne, in Co. Antrim (p. 25), while Hugh Hencken dug not only the crannog at Ballinderry, Co. Offaly (p. 152), but also the multiple-cist cairn at Poulawack, Co. Clare (p. 86). The same year, 1932, also saw the start of a series of excavations at northern megaliths, under the direction of Estyn Evans and the late Oliver Davies, which were to lead not only to a greater interest in, and understanding of, Irish megaliths, but also – in combination with the work of the Harvard Mission – to the emergence of a new generation of trained young Irish excavators. One of these was Seán P. Ó Ríordáin, at first Professor of Archaeology in Cork and later Macalister's successor in Dublin. He undertook an ambitious programme of excavation at Lough Gur in Co. Limerick, where he uncovered Neolithic houses in Ireland for the first time (p. 35), and subsequently he dug at the great royal site of Tara in Co. Meath (p. 187). But his spade ran ahead of his pen, and his untimely death in 1957 left some important work unpublished. Another young excavator was Joseph Raftery, later Director of the National Museum, who dug the tumulus cemetery at Carrowjames (p. 103) in the 1930s, one of the Loughcrew megaliths and the Rath of Feerwore (p. 158) in the 1940s, and crannogs at Rathtinaun, Co. Sligo (p. 152) in the 1950s.

Perhaps the most prolific excavator of that younger generation was Michael J. O'Kelly, Ó Ríordáin's successor in the Cork chair, and a great exponent of the art of practical archaeology. His excavations at sites of very considerable variety culminated in his thirteen seasons at Newgrange, meticulously published in a book which appeared only weeks after his death in 1982. George Eogan, the current holder of the chair of Archaeology in University College, Dublin, has been digging tirelessly for almost twice as many seasons at the neighbouring mound of Knowth, and has already produced two valuable monographs on his fascinating discoveries. But while Newgrange and Knowth have been the most demanding of recent excavations in terms of manpower and human commitment, rewarding advances in knowledge have been provided at a considerable variety of sites dug by other archaeologists, whose achievements will be noted in the ensuing chapters.

Excavation is undoubtedly the more newsworthy side of archaeology. Less glamorous and exciting, but equally necessary to a study of the country's past, is the work of surveying surviving monuments, be it in the form of De Valera and O Nualláin's *Survey of the Megalithic Tombs of Ireland*, or the more general surveys of specific areas such as Co. Donegal, the Dingle Peninsula or the Barony of Ikerrin. Worthy of mention here, too, are the series of county inventories recently initiated by the Commissioners of Public Works, of which those for counties Louth, Monaghan and Meath have already appeared. A valuable fillip has been given to this work by the aerial photography of J.K. St Joseph, of the Cambridge Aerial Survey, as well as by Leo Swan, and the evaluation of their results will, in time, bear even greater fruit than they have already.

The study of museum artefacts has been described as 10 per cent inspiration and 90 per cent perspiration, but it inevitably produces important results which have, in many cases, been summarized in the pages of this book. These can take the form of overviews of particular periods, as in the work of Peter Woodman (O'Kelly's successor in Cork) on the Mesolithic (Middle Stone Age), or extensive publications on selective material of a particular epoch, such as Barry Raftery's recent monographs on the objects of La Tène type surviving in Ireland. Rather than referring in this chapter to the other outstanding pieces of research on various specialized topics, it is felt preferable in a book of this length to summarize them in the appropriate place in the text which follows, and the reader will find the relevant publications listed in the bibliography.

# 2· The Search for the First Settlers

## The geographical setting

ON THE MAP OF EUROPE, Ireland can be seen to be a neat geographical entity tucked away up in the northwestern corner, the continental shelf's westernmost bastion against the force of the Atlantic waves. To the east it is cradled by the larger island of Britain, which separates it from – yet also links it with – France, the Low Countries and the European landmass in general. But in the same sense that 'no man is an island', the island of Ireland is not isolated either, for it has the advantage of being connected to its nearest neighbour by an easily navigable stretch of water, while at the same time preserving its individual identity by being separated from it.

Instead of having acted as a deterrent to people in reaching Ireland's shores, the sea has always served to attract both friend and foe to come and settle. It has helped the country to keep abreast of spiritual and physical developments elsewhere, thus providing a lifeline which, when severed, has been known to lead Ireland into an insularity noted for its cultural stagnation. In times past, the sea also provided a trade route with far-flung outposts along the Atlantic littoral. For all its apparent remoteness, Ireland curiously has a key position as being a half-way house along the whole of the Atlantic coast of Europe from Gibraltar to Norway. Although the distances are great even by today's standards, the sea-routes from the western coast of Iberia to Brittany and Ireland seem to have been familiar to navigators in prehistoric times, and today the traveller will find a certain similarity in the landscape of all of these three areas. With Scotland and the Orkneys as the connecting link, Ireland would seem to have been in contact, too, with the northern end of Europe, along routes which the Vikings were later to frequent.

Today, Ireland is 32,595 square miles in extent, with a population of just over 4 million. It is curiously comparable to a jagged-rimmed saucer in being flat in the middle, and rising gradually to various heights around the perimeter. The central plain consists largely of a limestone lowland, some of which is covered by bog. The hills around its periphery are of varying kinds. The oldest are the Caledonian granites and quartzites in Donegal, Mayo and Connemara which, together with those in Co. Down and in the southeast of the country, tend to run northeast-southwest in their foldings. Much of the northeastern county of Antrim is unusual in that it consists largely of basalt of volcanic origin. A large part of the southern province of Munster has a mainly sandstone base, with the mountains generally running in an east–west direction. The area between Dublin and Dundalk on the east coast provides an extensive break in the pattern of hills around the coast, which facilitated penetration of the country by incoming settlers.

Yet the physical appearance of the Ireland which we see today is a far cry from that which the earliest settlers encountered on their arrival – and even from that which pertained as late as the medieval period. The neat network of fields, divided by hedgerows or stone walls, and occasionally interrupted by small forests, is a creation of the last three centuries. Prior to AD 1600, the country was much more heavily wooded than it is today, but to find out what the face of the Irish landscape was like during prehistoric times, it is perhaps best to start our story by reverting back to the conditions prevailing long before people ever set foot on what is now the island of Ireland.

Throughout the Ice Age, 1,700,000–13,000 years ago, Ireland formed a part of the European Continent, but at various stages in its duration, much of the country was covered by an ice-cap of the kind one finds in Arctic areas today. The ice-cover was not, however, constant, for warm and cold stages alternating with one another caused the glaciers to retreat or expand accordingly. The last cold stage, known as the *Midlandian* because its glacial deposits are clearly visible in the midlands of Ireland, is thought to have set in about 75,000 years ago. At this time, central and northern parts of the country were completely ice-covered only for comparatively short periods, and the landscape was a tundra of the kind encountered, for instance, in northern Norway today, allowing a sparse plant life of sorts to develop on the mountain-tops. At the same period, some southern parts of the province of Munster would have been free of the crushing pressure of the heavy ice-cap, and there the woolly mammoth (*elephas primigenius*), brown bear (*ursus arctos*), arctic fox (*alopex lagopus*), the Irish giant deer (*megalocerus giganteus*) and the reindeer (*rangifer tarandus*) would have roamed or prowled in a landscape rich in grasslands and with occasional groups of birch or willow. It will come as a surprise to many to learn that the ice-bodies made their last expansional thrust southwards over much of Ireland as recently as about 15,000 years ago. But in the ensuing 2,000 years, decreasing amounts of snow caused stagnation and gradual disappearance of the ice-sheets, leaving, at first, a limited amount of plantlife of scattered herbs in an otherwise bare soil.

## The first peopling of Ireland

The question obviously arises as to whether people may have been present in Ireland during one or other of the warmer phases of the Ice Age when the glaciers were in retreat, perhaps at the same stage of the Palaeolithic or Old Stone Age period – some 20,000–15,000 years ago – when those wondrous animal paintings on cave walls in France and Spain were being

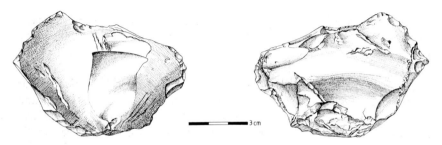

—— 3 cm

3 A Palaeolithic flint found at Mell, near Drogheda, Co. Louth.

done with a finesse which never fails to astound us today? Certain finds made during the last 100 years did raise hopes that it might be possible to answer the question with an enthusiastic affirmative. Earliest on the scene were the stones from Rosses's Point in Co. Sligo, which had the look of Old Stone Age tools until it was shown that their shapes were natural rather than man-made. Then there was the flint 'hand-axe' found in a crevice among the Iron Age *chevaux-de-frise* at Dún Aenghus on the Aran Islands, which is an undoubted Palaeolithic implement – but when or by whom it was brought to where it was found is anyone's guess! Professor Frank Mitchell, to whom Irish Mesolithic studies owe such a debt, found another piece of undoubted Palaeolithic flint-work at Mell, near 3 Drogheda, but it is in a different category altogether. This man-worked flint was found deep down in a quarry, probably dislodged from a layer perhaps a quarter of a million years old. Mitchell's interpretation was that it was a piece of Palaeolithic hunter's waste which had probably been deposited somewhere in the base of the Irish Sea before being brought by ice-movement to where he found it, and he concluded that it provided no firm evidence for the presence of Palaeolithic human populations in Ireland.

Caves in regions close to the south coast of Ireland which had been left untouched by the last Midlandian ice-advance were considered to be potentially hopeful locations for the discovery of Ice Age human habitation or shelter. For a while it looked as if the bones of a Palaeolithic man were going to be fleshed out at Kilgreany Cave, 5 miles from Dungarvan in Co. Waterford, which members of the Bristol Spelaeological Society had chosen for their investigative hunt in 1928. Here they found a human skull which they took to be associated with a hearth embedded in a stalagmite containing animal remains of a glacial type. But, because of the potentially crucial role which this skull could play in unravelling the history of Ireland's earliest people, the Harvard Archaeological Mission decided to re-excavate the cave in 1934 under the direction of Hallam L. Movius. He discovered that the cave deposits had, in fact, become somewhat mixed up, and that the skull had been buried in a pit which had been dug down from above into the Palaeolithic layer. This has been confirmed only very recently by a hitherto incompletely published radiocarbon date which showed conclusively that the skull belonged to the Neolithic, or New Stone Age, sometime between 3000 and 2500 bc – so exit our first serious contender for the role of Ireland's earliest known man. Genuine traces of Palaeolithic populations may yet be found in Ireland, but on present evidence it is likely that the first human foot to have trodden on Irish soil was about 4,000–5,000 years older than the Neolithic man from Kilgreany, but not as early as the last cold period of the Ice Age which came to an end around 11000 bc.

This cold period was quickly followed by an improvement in the climate which provided temperatures probably 1 or 2 degrees warmer than those prevailing today, and which allowed the Irish giant deer with its magnificent antlers to reach its maximum development. But its success was short-lived, because within about 2,000 years, around 9000 bc, a new severe cold phase set in which must have made it difficult, if not impossible, for this noble animal to survive. This time, however, the cold spell was of comparatively short duration, and 8000 bc, approximately, saw the opening of a warm phase which still persists today, and which is called the *Littletonian*, after a bog in Co. Tipperary where its history has been monitored in pollen. The higher temperatures encouraged warmth-loving plants and animals to invade Ireland once more, and provided an environment suitable for what was, on the basis of our present knowledge, probably the first human settlement of Ireland.

## Mesolithic hunters and gatherers

The question as to when the land link between Ireland and Britain was finally severed is one which has been hotly debated for decades, but there is now a growing consensus among scholars in favour of the existence of one or more land-bridges between Ireland and Britain for a sufficient length of time after the onset of the warm Littletonian phase for people to have arrived in Ireland across dry land. Some plants which expanded northwestwards from the European Continent, as the icy conditions retreated northwards, got across Britain to Ireland, while others made it only as far as Britain, presumably because the disappearance of the land-bridge made further progress to Ireland impossible. Richard Preece's recent discovery near Newlands Cross in Co. Dublin of the presence, around 5800 bc, of certain freshwater molluscs which were similar to contemporary examples in Wales, suggests that they pond-hopped their way to Ireland before the land-bridge was finally breached by the sea shortly afterwards. It was probably the breaking down of the land-bridge which prevented roe deer, wild cattle, otter and beaver from having reached Ireland, and which precociously deprived St Patrick of the credit which he subsequently received for having kept the country free of snakes.

The counting of plant and tree pollen in various levels of Littleton and other bogs has enabled us to gain an insight into the development of flora in the Irish landscape as the country gradually warmed up again at the opening of the Littletonian phase. At first, meadows appeared, to be joined shortly afterwards by juniper, which was quickly overshadowed by willows and birches, leading to the creation of Ireland's first post-glacial woodlands. By 7000 bc, hazel began to spread and engulf some of the other vegetation, and at the same time we find the pine tree gradually moving into Ireland. Copses of elm, oak, birch and – on damper ground – willow were also beginning to make their mark on the Irish skyline. The extensive forest and scrub cover would have been interrupted only by the water of lakes and river-channels, and it was these latter which provided the earliest inhabitants with the easiest means of penetrating into the interior of the country during the Mesolithic, about 7500–3300 bc.

Although the learned and ingenious seventeenth-century Irish archbishop James Ussher teased out from the Bible that the world was not created until the year 4004 BC, we now know that Ireland was already inhabited in the eighth millennium bc in radiocarbon years, or the ninth millennium BC in actual calendar years (Chapter 1). The earliest radiocarbon date we have for the probable presence of people in Ireland is perhaps that of *c*.7490 bc obtained recently by Swedish archaeologists at Woodpark in Co. Sligo where, however, the relationship between the charcoal sample and the primitive settlement there remains somewhat obscure.

But a much clearer picture begins to emerge at Mount Sandel in Co. Derry, a 30-m-high bluff overlooking the river Bann some miles upstream from the sea, which was excavated between 1973 and 1977 by Peter Woodman, whose work during the last fifteen years has revolutionized our views on the Irish Mesolithic. The radiocarbon dates which he obtained for the settlement there ranged from *c*.7010 bc to *c*.6490 bc. In the occupation levels spanning about 500 years, he found – contrary to all expectations – the remains of a number of roughly round houses about 6 m in diameter which are not only the oldest Mesolithic houses to be discovered in Ireland, but also pre-date any found in Britain. The visible traces of these houses were in the form of post-holes, rounded stains in the ground which had resulted from the decay of the timbers which the holes had once held. The post-holes, about 20 cm deep, were not absolutely vertical, but angled slightly inwards – suggesting that the houses had been dome-shaped and made of saplings bent inwards to meet at a joint in the centre of the roof, but without any central support. These saplings would probably have had lighter branches interwoven with them, in order to keep out the wind and rain. Because the interior of the houses had been cleared down to old ground level, it is possible that the surface sods had been removed and placed on the outside walls for further weatherproofing.

4

4–7 **The Mesolithic site of Mount Sandel, Co. Derry** (*Above*) Post-holes of a house. (*Opposite, top row*) Typical flint microliths from the site, left to right: scalene triangle for arrow tip(?); rod for food preparation(?); small knife; 'needle point'; and waste piece. (*Opposite, bottom two rows*) Larger flint tools, clockwise from top left: chopper; chisel or adze; pick; scraper; and an awl. (*Opposite, far right*) How projectile heads from Mount Sandel may have been mounted.

Inside the houses were hearths measuring about 1 m across, and about 30 cm deep. A number of small stake-holes around these hearths suggested that some form of simple structure had been set up around the fire for cooking purposes. The absence of wild cattle, roe deer and elk from Mesolithic Ireland meant a very reduced range of mammals which the people of Mount Sandel could have hunted. But from the discovery of duck, pigeon and grouse bones, as well as the remains of eels and fresh- and seawater fish such as salmon, sea bass and the occasional flounder, we may presume that the inhabitants of Mount Sandel did indeed spend considerable time fishing and hunting game to provide themselves with the necessary protein. In their hunt for pig and hare to augment their menu, they may have been accompanied by some form of dog, even then, apparently, man's best friend.

Both close to and slightly further away from the houses there was plenty of waste flint, but very few finished pieces. However, those which had been completed were very carefully worked, and they may have been thrown among the waste flakes when more suitable replacements for them became available. The flint used had been brought from some consider- able distance away, probably from the coast of Co. Antrim, where the plentiful supply present in the chalk outcrop may have been one of the major reasons why the prehistoric inhabitants were attracted to the

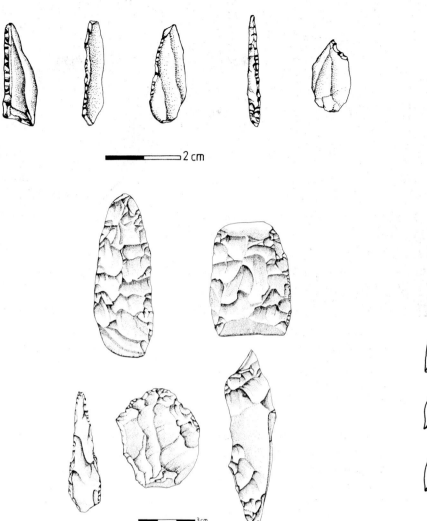

2 cm

3 cm

general area in the first place. Typical for the site were small narrow-bladed flint pieces called microliths, often in geometrical shapes such as the scalene triangle, as well as 'rods' and needle-points. Also found in some quantity were axes made of flint cores, that is, those from which other pieces may already have been detached, as well as small flint awls, scraping tools and blades, some of which bore traces of iron-pigment red ochre. Occasionally, up to ten similar pieces of worked flint were found together, suggesting that they may originally have been mounted together as 'projectile-heads'. One surprise on such an early site was the presence of a number of stone axes, as these axes were traditionally held not to have been introduced until the arrival of the first agriculturalists in the ensuing Neolithic. There is as yet, however, no convincing evidence that these stone axes were used for cutting down trees to clear the forest growth.

With the exception of the polished stone axes, most of the finished stone work from Mount Sandel was generally of a kind used by many other communities which would have hunted in the Stone Age forests in other parts of Northern Europe. Like them, too, the people of Mount Sandel were hunters and gatherers who may not have stayed in the same spot all the year round, but may have moved to other locations at certain times of year to obtain their hunting booty. The salmon bones from the site imply that Mount Sandel was inhabited during the summer, and a further autumn occupation is rendered probable because of the eels and the discovery of the remains of hazelnuts, the latter of which may have been stored, squirrel-like, for the winter. As the pigs on the site were apparently young when slaughtered, the inhabitants seem to have been there late in the winter, when other sources of food-supply would have become scarce. Indeed, of all the Mesolithic sites known in Ireland, Mount Sandel is the one which probably comes closest to being an all-the-year-round settlement.

Even had human bones been found, it would be difficult to estimate the size of the community which lived at any one time at Mount Sandel, but it is unlikely to have been more than about a dozen individuals. Members of this small group may have travelled some distance from the camp, or have traded with others who came from further south, as one material called chert – a substitute for flint found in the northern part of the Irish midlands – was discovered at Mount Sandel without any of the waste products normally associated with knapping on site, suggesting that it may have come from as far away as the midlands. Some of the smaller flint items, such as needle-points, microliths and broad-flake adzes, are of a kind not found outside Ireland, and from the presumption that it would probably have taken some time for these types to have gone through an indigenous development in Irish surroundings, Woodman concluded that the people who lived at Mount Sandel were not first-generation immigrants to Ireland, but that their forebears must already have been in the country for some reasonable period of time before the site was first settled.

Thirty years ago, almost all the known Irish Mesolithic sites had come to light in the northeast of the country, to a considerable extent because of the activities of collectors in the area around Belfast who were interested in filling their display cabinets at home with objects of antiquarian interest which were easy and cheap to come by, if you had an eye for finding them. But, in the meantime, Frank Mitchell has discovered a number of Mesolithic locations along the east coast as far south as Dublin Bay. He, and others, also brought to light further instances of Mesolithic stone-working in the Irish midlands. The traditional notion of the dominance of the northeastern counties of Antrim and Down during the early Mesolithic was dramatically altered with the National Museum's excavation at another newly discovered midland site – Lough Boora, near

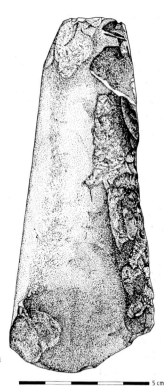

8 A ground stone axe-head from Lough Boora, Co. Offaly.

5 cm

Kilcormac in Co. Offaly. There, on the edge of a former lake which was later smothered by peat-bog, Michael Ryan unearthed the remains of a settlement which provided radiocarbon dates ranging from *c*.7030–*c*.6400 bc, obtained from charcoal in the somewhat informal hearths, showing it to be roughly contemporary with Mount Sandel. The Lough Boora soundings revealed up to 400 leaf-shaped or triangular blades and over 200 microliths which were closely comparable to the material from Mount Sandel. Here, too, polished stone axe-heads formed part of the assemblage though, among the flint work, there were fewer scalene triangles, needle-points and core-axes than at Mount Sandel. The ubiquity of nuts and the range of animal bones at Lough Boora also provided parallels for Mount Sandel, but the lack of houses makes Lough Boora look more like the remains of a temporary camp. Traces of the Irish giant deer were found embedded beneath the archaeologically fertile layers at Lough Boora, supporting the notion (see above) that this splendid animal had probably become extinct before the arrival of human populations in Ireland.

8

The stone used by the Lough Boora people was, however, different from most of that at Mount Sandel. Here it was the somewhat blacker chert which was used, small quantities of which were noted above as having also been present at Mount Sandel. The Lough Boora people may, indeed, have derived their chert from the same north midlands source which could have supplied Mount Sandel.

The revelations from Lough Boora, which now show that the Irish midlands were being penetrated at the same time as the Mount Sandel settlement was established, make it clear that we can no longer afford to envisage Ireland's earliest Mesolithic families as having come only to northeastern Ireland. The Lough Boora excavation, and Peter Woodman's recent discoveries of earlier Mesolithic flintwork in the valley of the Munster Blackwater, should prompt us to envisage Mesolithic people crossing what is now the Irish Sea by a number of land-bridges which were still in existence at the time, and arriving at various points in the present provinces of Ulster and Leinster, where some of their earliest settlements may have been submerged by the subsequent rise in sea-level.

If we try to pin-point an area from whence the earliest settlers are likely to have come, we are hampered by the lack of a closely comparable group of flint implements in Britain to guide us. The Isle of Man has, however, produced somewhat similar material, so that it is not unreasonable to suppose that it was from there, as well as from areas of northwestern England and southern Scotland, and probably also from Wales, that the earliest populations of Ireland may have come. But this lack of comparative material in Britain, and the seemingly developed nature of much of the early Mesolithic stonework found at Mount Sandel, Lough Boora and elsewhere, might indicate, as already suggested, that human populations had already been established in Ireland for some time, and had developed an individual range of tools and implements independent of the parent British groupings before they settled at Mount Sandel and Lough Boora. It would cause no surprise, therefore, if even earlier Mesolithic sites in Ireland were to be uncovered in the future.

The recently obtained radiocarbon dates which have made revolutionary changes in our understanding of Mesolithic Ireland show an as yet unfilled gap between the early Mesolithic of Mount Sandel and Lough Boora on the one hand, and the subsequent late Mesolithic on the other. We can only speculate as to whether the gap is real – that is, whether the early Mesolithic population may have died out sometime during the seventh millennium bc (like the Vikings in medieval Greenland) only to be replaced by new arrivals some hundreds of years later, or whether sites still to be discovered might help to fill the gap. Could it even be that the rupture of the land-bridge with Britain may have caused some stagnation in the now isolated Irish population, until such time as new stock plucked up the courage to cross the sea?

Around this time, the nature of the forest cover began to change. The richer midland soils came to be dominated by alder, oak and elm, though the birch and pine probably still flourished in the upland regions. But the climate, while still registering temperatures marginally above those of the present day, was becoming slightly wetter, and some land-surfaces began to be swamped, providing conditions suitable for the development of the earliest bogs. This may well have reduced the amount of open water available for fishing and, particularly in the midlands, have forced the population to settle near the larger rivers and lakes.

## The Late Mesolithic

The gap in our knowledge of human populations at the end of the early Mesolithic, mentioned above, coincided with a change in the technique by which stones were struck, from the use of a wooden or bone punch to one using a hammerstone. The nature of the stonework changed too, as Hallam Movius realized in his excavations at Curran Point in the 1930s. The predominant tool types of the late Mesolithic are the heavier blades, and flakes which bear considerable traces of trimming at their butts, including the so-called 'Bann flakes'. The small axes of the early Mesolithic are replaced by a series of axes which are either of larger proportions, or are polished. Heavy implements such as picks and borers also come into use. Many of these may well have been some kind of woodworking tools and, in contrast to the early Mesolithic, there is an absence of stones which can clearly be associated with hunting activities.

Newferry in Co. Antrim, located near Lough Beg at the northern end of Lough Neagh – Ireland's largest lake – provides us with the best opportunity for studying the late Mesolithic. A number of excavations have taken place in the area since Movius worked there in the 1930s, the most important of which is that at Site 3, investigated by Peter Woodman in 1970–71. Its real significance lies in the fact that its various layers provide us with a series of radiocarbon dates ranging from $c.6240$–$c.3465$ bc, which virtually covers the whole of the later Mesolithic and even continues into the earliest phases of the Neolithic. Unlike Mount Sandel, located further down the river Bann, its soil is so acidic that organic remains were not preserved. But this was more than compensated for by the very extensive collection of stonework which survived, showing a progression from a rather elongated blade to a shorter, broader type of blade. The presence in one of the oldest layers of a few microliths, and the occasional scraper and burin – which are more typical of the early Mesolithic – supports the notion that there was, in fact, some continuity in the population between the early and late Mesolithic. One of the surprising features of the stone tools found at Newferry 3 is that they betray little major change over a period of almost 3,000 years, suggesting that the people there continued to live in comparative isolation in the same area over a number of millennia. There is no obvious indication during this period of the arrival of additional groups from elsewhere, bringing with them new flint-knapping methods or different types of implements. Connections with the outside world and, more particularly, with Britain, would appear to have come to a virtual standstill, doubtless assisted by the land-bridge having been engulfed by the sea.

But even if external links across the sea had ground to a halt, the population within Ireland itself was probably on the move, at least in small numbers, particularly towards the end of the Mesolithic period. Considerable coastal activity can be seen at two sites at opposite ends of Dublin Bay – Sutton on the northern end, twice excavated by Frank Mitchell, and Dalkey Island on the southern end, investigated by David Liversage. Both produced shell middens, areas with concentrations of stoneworking and probable traces of settlement, as well as flint and chert of a kind similar to that from Newferry – heavy blades of Larnian type (a broad flint-blade called after the type-site at Larne in Co. Antrim), in addition to stone axes. Both were occupied at almost exactly the same time, to judge by the radiocarbon dates of c.3350 bc for Dalkey Island, and c.3300 bc for Sutton. But recent fieldwork and excavation has shown that Mesolithic populations also penetrated into the western part of Munster at the same time – even reaching the very end of the Dingle Peninsula. There, a small excavation by Peter Woodman at Ferriter's Cove produced radiocarbon dates ranging from c.3670–c.3240 bc for three separate but contiguous sites. Closely associated with material from one of the areas investigated was what may be a plano-convex knife of Neolithic type, and when taken in conjunction with pottery found in the youngest layers at Newferry 3, and a probable ox bone at Sutton – both signs of the Neolithic – we may take it that the last phases of the culture of these Mesolithic people were, as we shall see in the next chapter, contemporary with the earliest traces of agricultural activity in the Neolithic, which is likely to have seen a new influx of people into Ireland. The old, established Mesolithic folk, instead of being exterminated, were in all likelihood gradually assimilated into the newly arrived population groups, adopting their more settled way of life, and possibly exchanging the fish they were so expert in catching for stone axes perhaps, and also possibly for the meat of domesticated animals which the newcomers could offer.

No skeletal remains can be recognized as belonging to these Mesolithic people who, in the present state of our knowledge, were the first to populate Ireland. We can say in all probability, however, that the makers of the stone implements described above represent the basic human stock onto whose blood-gene pool all subsequent peoples were 'grafted', so that they may truly be described as the first Irish men and women, the ancestors of the Irish people of today.

# 3·Farmers and Megalith-builders

## The arrival of farming

AFTER THE COLONIZATION by human populations, perhaps the most important and long-lasting change in Ireland before the coming of Christianity was one which took place almost mid-way between the two events – the introduction of agriculture and sedentary life, a great step forward which was to usher in the second, slightly longer, half of the prehistory of Ireland. This incisive alteration in the life-style of the country's inhabitants, which heralded the start of the Neolithic period during the fourth millennium BC, had its origins more than 3,000 years earlier in the countries bordering the biblical lands of the Near East which, together with China, were the source of so many innovations in the world's history. The right conditions had prevailed in the Fertile Crescent – the relatively well-watered band of land stretching in an arc from Palestine to Iraq – for people to cultivate crops, and with these first steps in agriculture came the desirable necessity of settling close to the planted fields, thus paving the way for the development of villages and, later, large and powerful towns. The concomitant domestication of certain animal species provided resident protein without having to go hunting for it. It was not long before the advantages of the new settled way of life were blazoned far beyond the bounds of Mesopotamia, and knowledge of agriculture spread gradually to Europe along two very different routes – one by land along the Danube into Central and Northwestern Europe, the other by sea across the Mediterranean to Spain and France as far as the Straits of Dover.

Neither a broad stretch of water such as the English Channel, nor dense forest cover, obstructed Neolithic populations in their search for land suitable for cultivation and stock-raising. Undaunted by the primeval forest which blocked progress towards Northwestern Europe, trees were cleared where necessary to provide living space, and also fodder for cattle. This land-clearance can be monitored by studying the relative numbers of pollen retrieved from successive layers of bog or moist ground, a technique pioneered by the Danes and adapted to Irish conditions by Frank Mitchell and others. In its earlier stages, pollen analysis was dependent upon the finding of archaeologically dated artefacts in the various strata in order to find out the relative dates at which changes occurred in the pollen spectrum – and therefore in the landscape. But, in recent decades, the method has reached a much greater degree of refinement by the provision of radiocarbon dates from the separate layers without having to rely on the haphazard finding of archaeological material in them.

The achievement of this refined chronology has demonstrated that, sometime before the end of the fourth millennium bc, elm trees showed a decline in numbers throughout many parts of Europe, including Ireland. Something like the Dutch elm disease, which has recently been decimating the stocks of this tree in Europe and beyond, has been given as one possible reason for the reduction in numbers. An alternative explanation is that the decline may be seen in conjunction with land-clearance in the early part of the Neolithic period. This could have been brought about either by cattle eating the bark and thereby killing the parent tree, or by settlers felling the tree or at least killing it by removing a ring of its bark, in order to create more grazing land for cattle, or more arable land for crops. Whatever the reason for the elm decline, it need no longer be equated with the first signs of people clearing the post-glacial forests of Ireland, as a number of scholars believed, although this may have exacerbated it. It is now becoming evident that clearance of woodland, in advance of cereal cultivation, may have begun some considerable time before the elm decline in the later centuries of the fourth millennium bc. The earliest possible date provided so far for this clearance in Ireland comes, almost unexpectedly, from the southwestern part of the country. At Cashelkeelty in Co. Kerry, Ann Lynch examined the stratified pollen and found a considerable reduction in the total percentage of tree pollen at some period between c.3895 and c.2965 bc. This reduction may have been caused by slashing and burning the trees, as suggested by the finding of charcoal, followed immediately by the cultivation of wheat and barley accompanied by the presence of ribwort plantain (*plantago lanceolata*) – a tell-tale sign of human cultivation – and giving way later to pasturage before the wood finally regenerated again. As yet we cannot find any archaeological traces of the people responsible for this agricultural activity, nor can we say where they are likely to have come from or what subsequently became of this community.

That this agricultural activity in the southwest of the country was neither a chimaera nor a flash in the pan is demonstrated by the recurrence of similar findings in the extreme opposite end of the island at roughly the same time. At Ballyscullion in Co. Antrim, the pollen gave clear indications of human interference with the tree cover between c.3865 and c.3580 bc, and a slightly later period saw an increase in grass and ribwort plantain pollen. But, unlike Co. Kerry so far, northern Ireland has been able to produce archaeological evidence of human activity to accompany the tree decline in the pollen record. This comes from Ballynagilly near Cookstown, in Co. Tyrone, where Arthur ApSimon excavated an Early Neolithic settlement in 1969. The settlement measured at least 60 m across, and it included pits containing pottery ranging in date from c.3795–c.3550 bc.

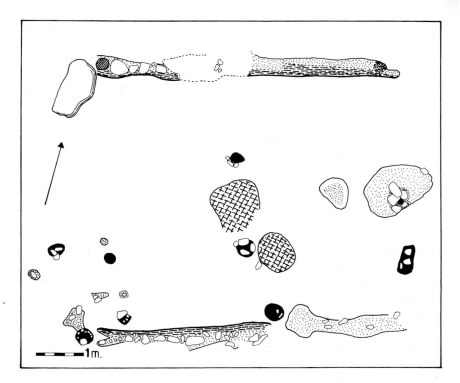

9 Plan of the Neolithic house at Ballynagilly, Co. Tyrone.

But the most important discovery at this settlement at Ballynagilly was 9
a wooden house, the oldest known Neolithic house in Britain or Ireland. It
was situated on the crown of a hill over 200 m high, a location explained by
the warmer climate prevailing at the time, which permitted agriculture at
higher levels than is practicable today. The house itself was almost square
in shape, measuring about 6.5 m by 6 m, orientated east-west, and thus
little different in floor-area from some of the more rectangular modern
vernacular houses in the locality. To facilitate the making of the long
walls, a trench 30–40 cm wide and 20–30 cm deep was dug, and into it
planks of radially split oakwood were placed upright to form the house
wall. The house was subsequently destroyed by fire, but this enabled the
excavator to retrieve some charcoal which provided a radiocarbon date of
c.3215 bc. Traces of post-holes gave a less clear indication of the position
of the east and west walls of the house, which may not have been planked
as the north and south walls had been. The house had two hearths, one
bowl-shaped and filled with burnt material, the other an area of clay
burned red. There was also a small pit containing potsherds, and further
pottery fragments were found along with flint implements inside and
outside the house.

A plank-walled house of Ballynagilly type – unique for Ireland when it was discovered – makes us look for its ultimate origin towards Central Europe, where such houses are found associated with the Linear Pottery culture of the fifth millennium bc onwards. These continental settlements had already developed into sizeable village communities, but when farmers finally crossed the English Channel, they probably split into smaller family groups so that, in Britain and Ireland, the isolated house seems to have become the norm, as at Ballynagilly.

The date of the Ballynagilly house shows that it is roughly contemporary with – or only marginally later than – the latest phases of the Mesolithic, as we saw in the last chapter. Ballynagilly is also only slightly later than the first record we have for the probable presence of domesticated cattle and possibly also sheep or goat in Ireland – at Ringneill Quay, Co. Down, datable to $c.3430$ bc. While pig was also present in the earlier Mesolithic at Mount Sandel, it would seem that ox and the first sheep or goats were probably introduced as domesticates into Ireland at the beginning of the Neolithic, as they do not seem to have been present there in a wild state at any earlier stage. Because the inhabitants of the Late Mesolithic midden at Sutton seem to have known of the existence of the ox, it is possible that the Late Mesolithic inhabitants introduced cattle into the country, but it is more likely that cattle and sheep were introduced in an already domesticated state by intrusive Neolithic peoples, including the not-too-remote ancestors of the Ballynagilly house-builders, probably from somewhere in the northern half of Britain. These people would probably have practised a mixed tillage/pastoral economy, growing wheat and barley (whose seed impressions have been found on Neolithic pottery), preferably on light upland soils where cultivation and forest-clearance would have been easier than on the heavier lowland clays. Ireland was more than large enough to give adequate living space for these new Neolithic agriculturalists to practise their farming at the same time as the Mesolithic peoples continued their hunting expeditions until – probably after some centuries – they were assimilated with the Neolithic stock, and farming became the main method for producing food.

We need not think of any large-scale 'invasions' of these Neolithic people into Ireland. Their arrival would have been gradual, and would probably have involved small groups coming into the country over a considerable period of time, some of them possibly attracted to it by the fish along its coasts. But one could imagine that the way in which they came to Ireland might have corresponded to the model proposed for England by Humphrey Case. He envisaged that, while the crops were ripening during the summer, a group of scouts would have been sent out in boats to prospect for suitable settling grounds, reporting back on potential living conditions. After the crops were harvested, sometime between August and November, the small family groups would then cross the sea, carrying with them their breeding and milking livestock as well as seed-corn from the recent crop. The boats used may not have been much longer or bigger than the canvas-covered currachs still used for similar purposes along the west coast of Ireland today. It would not have been easy for cattle, lying down with their legs tethered, to survive a sea-crossing of more than a few days, and it would not be unreasonable, therefore, to assume that many of the earliest Neolithic settlers may have come from southwestern Scotland to counties Antrim and Down, which were easily visible across the North Channel. However, more intrepid communities may also have made the longer crossing further south in the Irish Sea.

Their first scouting parties may have sought out areas with plenty of elm which indicate rich and fertile soils, and, once arrived, the groups would have collected twigs and leaves to provide the cattle with fodder for the first crucial winter. Later, they would have set about felling some of the elm – and probably also oak – to provide space for agriculture between the stumps. The widespread hazel may also have been partially cleared. Although, as we have seen, traces of people disturbing the natural forest cover in Ireland emerge at least a few centuries earlier than the construction of the Ballynagilly house, it is nevertheless interesting to note that building activity at Ballynagilly is roughly contemporary with the decline in elm seen in the pollen diagrams for the centuries leading up to 3000 bc.

Trees would have been felled with the aid of stone axes of a kind formerly considered to have been first introduced in the Neolithic period, but which can now be seen to have already been in use in Ireland during the Mesolithic, as Mount Sandel and Lough Boora have shown. These stone axes would have been mounted at right angles to a wooden shaft, and experiments in Denmark have demonstrated that it takes less than an hour to cut down a medium-sized tree with such an axe. The stone preferred for these axes was porcellanite, and fieldworkers have discovered two 'factories' in northern Ireland where these axes were made – one at Tievebulliagh in Co. Antrim, and the other on the off-shore island of Rathlin in the same county. Probably some time during the third millennium bc, these axe 'factories' must have become quite specialized in the making and marketing of polished stone axes, for their products were widely distributed throughout Ireland – and also in Scotland and 10 Britain. It was presumably not only the porcellanite axes which were used for forest-clearance. The northern Irish flint, which had proved to have such a magnetic attraction for the Mesolithic population, was also put to good use by the Neolithic farmers in the making of hollow scrapers (a typically Irish implement) which could have been used for stripping bark, and also in the preparation of arrows and javelins which would have been fitted out with lozenge-shaped flint arrowheads for hunting purposes.

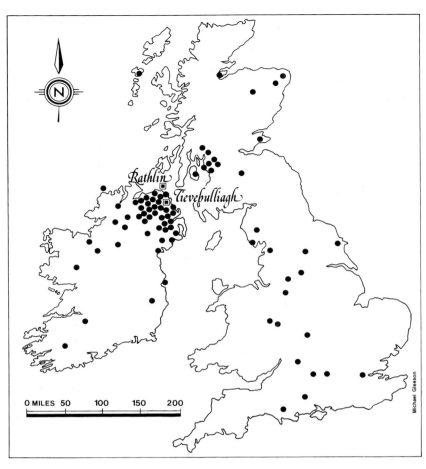

10 Distribution in the British Isles of Neolithic axes from Tievebulliagh and Rathlin, Co. Antrim.

The land thus cleared, and then cultivated by mattock, may have quickly lost its fertility, but once the Neolithic farming communities established a foothold in Ireland, it would not have proved difficult to search out new potential pastures and land for tillage. However, the pollen diagrams show that within some hundreds of years after the original forest-clearances, the woodlands regenerated, even though they did not entirely regain their original strength.

## Neolithic houses and field systems

When the planked house was excavated at Ballynagilly in 1969, it was as unique as it was unexpected in Ireland. But, by a curious coincidence, a somewhat similar house was brought to light during the following three years by Seán Ó Nualláin's excavations at Ballyglass in Co. Mayo. This house was about 15 m long and 6 m wide, and was orientated southeast-northwest. As was also the case with the Ballynagilly house, the walls had

had trenches prepared for them, but here they contained holes for upright posts which were seemingly joined by planks, of which some traces were found. The Ballyglass house had three parallel series of post-holes at the northwestern end, and a small narrow rectangular room at the opposite end.

The Ballyglass house was located at the northwestern end of a court 11 cairn, a type of megalithic monument which will be discussed in greater detail below. As the excavator remarked, 'it is difficult to avoid the conclusion that the house was intentionally demolished to make way for the construction of the tomb'. Fire-reddened areas of clay were found in both the principal and subsidiary rooms of the house. It might be tempting to view the house as having been a 'temple' associated with some ritual requirement before the erection of the court cairn, or even as a structure where the dead were placed for de-fleshing before the bones were given a final resting place, but we cannot be sure whether the house had a domestic or ritual function. Neolithic pottery and flint implements were found, though, owing to a lack of stratigraphical evidence, it is difficult to know which material belonged to the house and which to the court cairn. The charred wooden remains in the house foundation-trenches, which also contained pottery, produced a number of radiocarbon dates of which the earliest was *c.*2730 bc, showing that this house was about half a millennium later than that at Ballynagilly. One of two domestic structures in the forecourt of a second court cairn in the same townland gave radiocarbon dates a few hundred years later again.

11 Aerial view of the excavations at the central court cairn at Ballyglass, Co. Mayo, with the Neolithic house adjoining it.

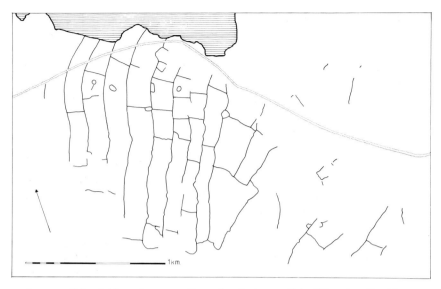

12 Layout of the fields and stone walls under the bog at Behy/Glenulra, Co. Mayo, as unearthed by 1985.

We are fortunate that, in other parts of north Mayo, bogs successfully covered not only court cairns, but also Neolithic field systems delimited by stone and earthen walls, which have only recently come to light with the extensive modern exploitation of the bogs. In his work on these field systems, which is still in progress, Seamus Caulfield has concentrated on two separate areas. One of these was at Belderg Beg, where sizeable but irregular stone walls were built before the bog started to grow. The outer rings of one pine tree which lived after the commencement of bog growth gave a radiocarbon date of c.2270 bc, suggesting that the field fences were somewhat older, though just how much older we do not know. The finding of Neolithic pottery, flints and a polished stone axe-head helped to confirm a Neolithic date for the first settlement, but, because there was no stratigraphical evidence, the relationship of the field fences to a round house which was also found could not be established. In this complex, Caulfield also discovered marks made perhaps by a primitive predecessor of the plough, together with cultivation ridges comparable to the nineteenth-century 'lazy beds' still visible on many upland locations in Ireland today. Michael Herity found similar traces at Carrownaglogh in the neighbouring county of Sligo, and fieldwork in recent decades has brought to light further examples of pre-bog walls in northern Ireland and as far south as Co. Kerry.

12    A better picture was gained at Caulfield's second site – Behy/Glenulra, 4 miles to the east, where the fences actually surrounded a court cairn at Behy. Here, roughly parallel walls of stone, 150–200 m apart, were found running inland from the coast for at least 800 m, with cross-walls dividing

the strips ladder-like into fields with a maximum extent of 7 hectares, or about 17 acres. An enclosure in one of the fields provided a terminal radiocarbon date of c.2510 bc, and the finds proved to be similar to those at Belderg Beg. The fields would appear to have been planned in one single operation, and may have been used for the enclosure of animals rather than for the protection of arable land. Even if beef production at the time were only half that of today's grasslands, Caulfield reckoned that four or five families could have been supported by 1 square km (0.4 square miles) of land there. The proximity to the Behy megalith makes it likely, of course, that the fields were laid out by the same people who built the cairn, and it also hints at a greater permanence of settlement than that of the first Neolithic arrivals in the fourth millennium bc, who may have had to make frequent moves to new locations once the ground they had originally tilled had become exhausted.

The first Neolithic houses which were in fact identified as such in Ireland were those excavated by Seán P. Ó Ríordáin around Lough Gur, 13 an area of southeast Limerick where the richness of prehistoric and later finds is testimony to the attractiveness of its limestone soils for generations of farmers and pastoralists. The Neolithic inhabitants chose slightly elevated sites for their (not necessarily contemporary) houses on the side of a hill called Knockadoon, overlooking the lake. One of these houses, at what is known as Circle L, gave a radiocarbon date of c.2740 bc, which would make it roughly contemporary with that at Ballyglass. But the Lough Gur houses differed structurally from those at Ballynagilly and Ballyglass, for they seem to have lacked the plank walls. Instead, some of the houses had a stone foundation for the walls, and the post-holes found at intervals along these foundations suggested that the walls were made of wattle-and-daub packed between the posts and on top of the stone foundations. One house, at Site A, was rectangular in shape, measuring 14 inside about 10 m by 6 m, and with an entrance at the southwestern corner, which is unusual. A series of internal post-holes at right angles to one another presumably supported purlins to steady the rafters, which were probably covered with thatch. Lough Gur also provides our first contact with the round house – a type which was to continue in use well into Christian times. The round houses at Lough Gur were also constructed with posts and wattle-and-daub, and they probably had a thatched roof.

Many other traces of human activity from the Neolithic period have come to light in excavated sites which have not, however, produced larger houses of the kind encountered hitherto. In Co. Sligo, Göran Burenhult and his interdisciplinary team of scientists have uncovered round huts on the slopes of Knocknarea which have given radiocarbon dates of c.2525 and c.2300 bc, while Neolithic kitchen middens in the same general locality gave dates ranging from c.2760–c.2020 bc, and even later. Other sites, such as Feltrim Hill in Co. Dublin, excavated by Patrick Hartnett

13,14 **Neolithic houses at Lough Gur, Co. Limerick** (*Above*) View of the lake in 1946, with house foundations visible in the foreground. (*Below*) Reconstruction of a round and a rectangular house from the site.

and George Eogan, and two separate sites at Townleyhall, Co. Louth, dug by David Liversage and George Eogan respectively, produced Neolithic material, including pottery, though no house foundations were recovered. A passage-tomb was found to have been built over one of the Townleyhall sites.

But there are also other intriguing places which have produced clear evidence of a Neolithic presence, without it being easy to determine the nature of the activity which caused it. One of these was Lyles Hill, a 15 hill-top site near Belfast excavated by Estyn Evans in 1937–38. At around the 700 ft (213 m) contour, the hill was surrounded by a low earthwork 10 m wide and 60–90 cm high, with a ditch neither inside nor outside it, and surrounding an area of 5 hectares or about 12½ acres. Inside was a cairn of stones and earth which had a great quantity of Neolithic pottery both in and underneath it, but no visible trace of any house was found.

Another Antrim hill-site, Donegore, is in the process of excavation by the Canadian archaeologist, James Mallory. This hill which, in comparison, is only about 80 m high, is surrounded by an inner and an outer ditch containing Neolithic pottery. But while this enclosure also had a mound inside, the ditches at Donegore are interrupted rather than continuous, giving rise to the comparison with the famous causewayed camps of southern England. Waste flake material found in the excavation suggests that the site was used for some industrial activity during the Stone Age.

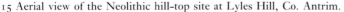

15 Aerial view of the Neolithic hill-top site at Lyles Hill, Co. Antrim.

One possible house-foundation – of slightly uncertain date – has been unearthed, but the real purpose of such an enigmatic site remains obscure. Was it a central meeting-place and fair-ground for the surrounding population, or had it some ritual purpose connected with burial, as the cairn might indicate? Perhaps the further excavation which is in progress may help to clarify this potentially exciting hill-top mystery.

One site which certainly would appear to have been of a ritual nature is that at Goodland, also in Co. Antrim. Here, too, there was a much smaller enclosure ditch, filled in shortly after it was made, and containing forty-four deposits which had been incorporated into the soil-filling. The ditch enclosed 171 pits and numerous stake-holes, giving dates in the second half of the third millennium. As the filling-in of the ditch was followed shortly afterwards by cultivation, and the minimum of 266 broken pots and numerous pieces of flint gave the impression of having been scraped up from scattered and abandoned settlement remains – of a kind which the people of the time may have seen to produce better crops subsequently on the site – the excavator, Humphrey Case, concluded that the remains were deposited as some sort of sympathetic magic associated in the minds of those who deposited them with fertile soil and improved cultivation.

### Potsherds and pot-types

The various sites discussed in this chapter have produced a bewildering number and variety of pots – the result of more than a millennium of potting activity. In the days before earthen pots were built up on the revolving wheel, and every pot was formed individually by hand alone, it followed that each one was different – with its own separate outline and thickness. When you add to this the fact that there are not even a dozen virtually complete Neolithic vessels known from Ireland, and that almost all survive in the form of a number of potsherds, it will be appreciated how difficult it is to create a binding classification of Irish Neolithic pottery.

The most straightforward, and probably also the earliest, type is the 'Western Neolithic' ware, so-called because of its widespread distribution over many parts of Western Europe, before its successors divided into many separate and differing regional styles. In Ireland, this type of pottery consists of round-bottomed bowls made of hard, darkish brown ware, with a noticeable shoulder where the upper and lower parts of the pot meet. The bowls have a variety of usually well-moulded neck forms turning outwards or inwards, and with pointed, rolled or T-shaped rims. There are a number of variants, sometimes regional in nature, which Humphrey Case denominated as the Dunmurry, Ballymarlagh, Lyles Hill and Limerick styles. This last-named encompasses the material from Lough Gur, Ó Ríordáin's Types I and Ia, whereby Ia is more decorative, with the addition of hatched lines to the rims. 'Western Neolithic' ware is the most common pottery type found on the excavated settlement sites

16

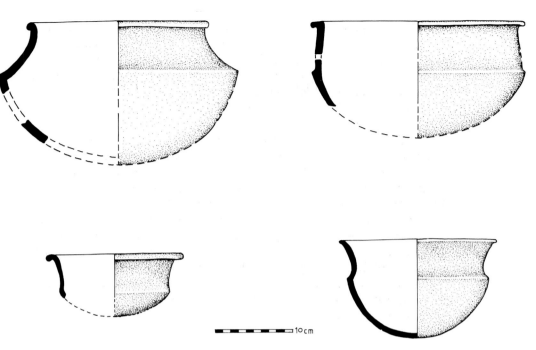

16 Undecorated Neolithic pottery, in Case's classification: top left, Dunmurry style (from Ballybriest); top right, Limerick style (from Lough Gur); bottom left, Ballymarlagh style (from Clontygora Small); bottom right, Lyles Hill style (from Ballyutoag).

such as Lough Gur, Lyles Hill and Ballynagilly, though it is also found in court cairns. Its better chances of preservation in the tombs, however, probably masks its more widespread use on habitations which have yet to be discovered, let alone excavated, and where it is likely to have been atomised into much smaller fragments. The solid simplicity of this ware is Neolithic society's visiting card, announcing its 'arrival' in a settled state after several millennia of nomadic wandering during the Mesolithic. The improved cooking and storage facilities which the pots provided, and the endless hours of toil which went into their making, are the proudly visible signs of the recently raised standards for the living, and a new status symbol for expressing extra respect for the dead.

The perceived importance of this pottery is underlined even more by the addition of ornament to a variety of Irish Neolithic wares which may vary in texture, but which often have a shape broadly similar to that of their plainer counterparts. These decorated wares have been studied and classified particularly by Case and Herity. Herity's first type may be described as a bipartite bowl with a constricted neck or, simply, a necked vessel, corresponding to some of Case's Ballyalton bowls. This group Herity further divided into three subgroups, of which the first has a low, in–turning section above the shoulder, and with overall channelled decoration either in straight lines laid out in a quadrupartite scheme, often with ladder–motifs, or in curves, with the channels meeting at an obtuse angle. Lugs are occasionally present. This subgroup is typically found in single burials. The second subgroup has a simpler rim, and the part above the shoulder rises inwards at a higher angle than in the case of the first subgroup. The decoration, usually on the upper half of the pot, may consist of a hurdle–pattern or a combination of radial or horizontal lines on the neck, and plain vertical channels or incised lines on the body of the pot. This subgroup is found in portal–tombs and court cairns, as well as on settlement and ritual sites. The third subgroup, a small one, has a longer and more upright neck, and the decoration consists of vertically channelled lines. It occurs mainly in court cairns.

Herity's second major group consists of broad–rimmed vessels, often with circumferential channelling with vertical incised lines or ladder–patterns on the characteristically broad rims. The body–shape of these round–bottomed bowls varies considerably, and the pots are found both in tombs and on habitation sites. Under the various names of Dundrum bowls, Murlough bowls and Sandhills Western, they belong to Case's overall classification of Sandhills ware which, as the name implies, occurs on coastal sites, though also found inland.

Under this umbrella–term Case also included what he called Goodland bowls, after the type–site mentioned above, but which Herity classed separately as his third major group, which he called Globular Bowls. The walls of these bowls turn into a pointed rim, below which are horizontal whipcord lines or chevron designs, which may be of finer or coarser execution. This group is found on a wide variety of sites. Herity's fourth group, which includes some of Case's Ballyalton bowls, are high–walled 'exotics' and hybrids, with vertical or horizontal decoration, or a combination of both, and which sometimes have lugs. Their occurrence is restricted to court cairns.

A very different type of pottery, formerly known as Loughcrew ware and now generally called Carrowkeel ware, is a simple semiglobular, thick–walled, rough pot decorated with often crude stab–and–drag ornament, made by a stick or bird–bone being pressed into the clay, and then dragged lightly until the next stab is made. Occasionally, patterns can be created which correspond to those on pottery from megalithic tombs outside Ireland, and it is not surprising therefore that Carrowkeel ware is found essentially in passage–tombs (see below), though it has occasionally been unearthed on settlement and ritual sites. No single explanation can be given for the use of all of these Neolithic pots, nor are we in a position to say what the significance may be of the various kinds of ornament used on the decorated pots.

18

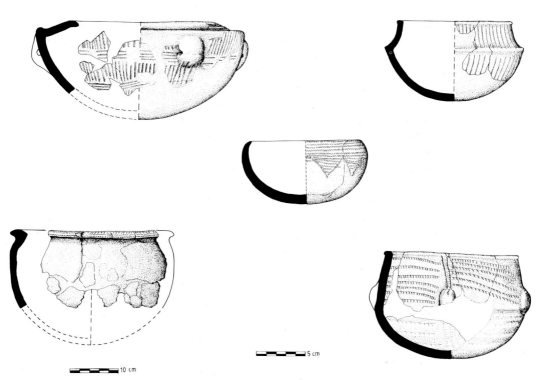

17 Decorated Neolithic pottery: top left, Ballykeel, Co. Armagh; top right, Ballyutoag, Co. Antrim; centre, Tamnyrankin, Co. Derry; bottom left, Townleyhall, Co. Louth; bottom right, Ballyalton, Co. Down (5-cm scale applies to all except bottom left).

18 An example of Carrowkeel ware, a pot from Monknewtown, Co. Meath. Ht 7.5 cm.

## Megalithic monuments

Newgrange, now famous for its orientation to the midwinter sunrise, is undoubtedly Ireland's best-known megalithic monument, but it is sometimes overlooked that it is only one of more than 1,200 megaliths in Ireland. These get their name from two Greek words *mega* and *lithos* – large stone. The description is well deserved, for these structures are often made with large and heavy stones, one of which – the capstone of Browneshill portal-tomb in Co. Carlow – is reputed to weigh 100 tonnes. Down the years, these megaliths have been called by many names – druids' altars, dolmens, cromlechs, giants' graves and Diarmuid and Gráinne's beds – this last associating them with the hastily erected, nocturnal refuges of the legendary couple who slept in a different place each night in their flight from the wrath of a jealous and ageing king. But not even the most optimistic giant could have hoped to build a megalith a day, and Newgrange, for instance, is so large that it may have taken anything up to thirty years to build it, according to one considered estimate.

Only a small percentage of Irish megaliths have been excavated, and as only a certain number yielded evidence of having contained human bones, it is by no means sure whether all megaliths in Ireland functioned as tombs. However, we know that many of them did, in fact, serve as communal burial places, as was doubtless also the case with thousands of other megaliths spread over wide areas of Western and Northern Europe, from Spain to Scandinavia.

Despite varying nomenclature, it is now generally recognized that – with the exception of some unclassifiable monuments – the Irish megaliths may be grouped into four major types as follows:

19

*Court cairns* in a long mound, with a forecourt at one end leading into a long and often subdivided chamber, though considerable variations of this basic plan are known. A total of 329 examples have hitherto been recognized.

*Portal-tombs or -chambers*, of which 161 are known, consisting of a number of upright stones covered by one or two capstones, and sometimes placed in a long or round mound. In order to avoid confusion, the portal-tomb is the term now generally preferred to describe what, in popular parlance, are more commonly called dolmens.

*Passage-tombs*, existing in anything up to 300 examples. These are round mounds having, roughly in the centre, a burial chamber which is reached by a passage leading in from the edge of the mound.

*Wedge-tombs*, which have long, rectangular burial chambers usually roofed with large stones, and placed in a long, wedge-shaped mound. The chamber tends to rise in height towards the front, and 387 of these tombs are known.

Although we know that the Vikings visited some of the tombs in the Boyne Valley in the ninth century AD, doubtless in pursuit of probably

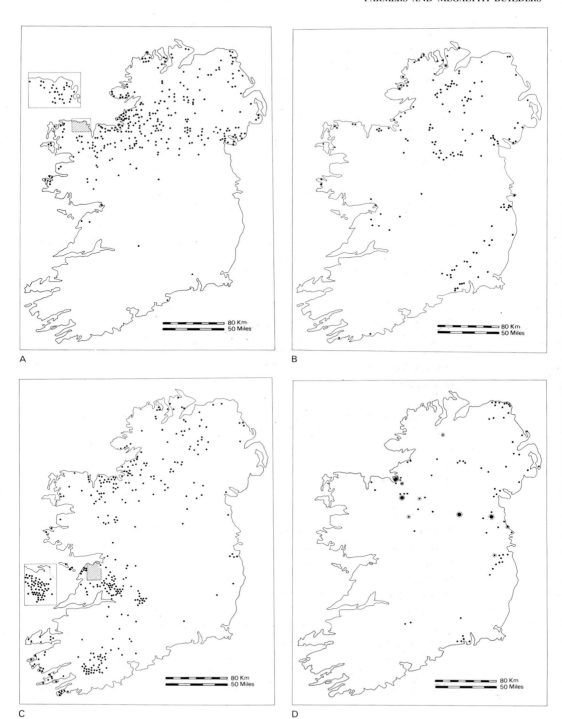

19 Distribution maps of the four kinds of megalithic tomb. (A) court cairns; (B) portal tombs; (C) wedge-tombs; (D) passage-tombs.

non-existent treasure, it was not until much more recent times that a number of tombs – such as Dowth and Carrowmore – became the subject of antiquarian research, though this often took the form of ransacking the chambers in search of objects to fill the display cases of the dilettanti. It was only in our own century that scientific excavations were carried out in order to provide us with a better picture of those who built these monuments. Half a century ago, less than a dozen court cairns were known to archaeologists, but patient surveying in recent decades has shown now that more than twenty times that number survive. Initial research in the 1930s concentrated on the court cairns in the north of Ireland, but in more recent years the field has been dominated by the large-scale excavations of passage-tombs, involving many seasons of digging.

During the last three decades, Ruaidhrí de Valera and others built up a widely held view of megalithic tombs which envisaged them as having been constructed by three separate invasions of peoples – probably from France. The first of these were seen as being the first Neolithic farmers, indeed almost the initial inhabitants of the country although, of course, we now know that human colonization of Ireland probably took place 3,500 years before a cow was milked, a cereal cultivated or a megalith built there. These people were considered to have landed in Co. Mayo where they constructed the first court cairns before moving on first into Ulster, and ultimately across the North Channel to Scotland. Portal-tombs were considered to be a local offshoot of the court cairns. The second group of invaders were thought to have come from Brittany up the Irish Sea, making a landing near the mouth of the river Boyne, where they built Newgrange, Knowth and Dowth before heading westwards via Loughcrew to Co. Sligo. The final group of invaders were envisaged as having landed on the south coast, where they started building wedge-tombs, before spreading further northwards. The court cairns were seen as being the earliest megaliths, followed some considerable time later by the passage-tombs, while the wedge-tombs were thought to have been built in the Bronze Age.

Thirty years ago, Stuart Piggott saw most of the tombs as having been erected during the second millennium BC. But during the last two decades in particular, a veritable revolution has been taking place in our understanding of Irish megalithic monuments which involves a radical reassessment of 'traditional' views. This revolution has been brought about firstly by the accumulation of a considerable number of radiocarbon dates for some of the megaliths, and secondly by some recent excavations, including those carried out by a Swedish group at Carrowmore during the years 1977–79.

Carrowmore is a megalithic cemetery spread out over a large area of flattish land some 3 miles west of Sligo town. In the last century, it consisted of over 100 monuments, but gravel digging has sadly reduced that number to less than a third of its former strength – a grievous loss when we consider that, in its original state, Carrowmore was perhaps the largest megalithic cemetery in the whole of Europe. Four of the surviving monuments were excavated by the Swedish team under Göran Burenhult. One of these was Grave 7 – a megalith with a polygonal chamber of five stones supporting a large capstone, and with two further additional stones at the entrance. It stood at the centre of a circle of thirty-one glacial boulders, and appears to have had no mound covering it originally. Most of the material in the chamber was found to have been disturbed, but four intact cremation burials were discovered between the upright stones. In the centre of the chamber was a post-hole which was deemed to have been part of the original construction, and it provided a radiocarbon date of $c.$3290 bc. However, because of the uncertain connection between post-hole and stone tomb, some doubt has been cast on the acceptability of the radiocarbon determination for the dating of the tomb.

Grave 27, one of the largest surviving monuments of the Carrowmore cemetery, was also excavated by Burenhult. It, too, had a stone circle surrounding it, though of larger dimensions. At its centre was a cross-shaped chamber without any passage leading into it (see below). This central chamber had been disturbed many times, even during the prehistoric period, but the refill material in the chamber and that from the

26

20

20 Montage of Grave 27, Carrowmore, Co. Sligo, seen from above during excavation.

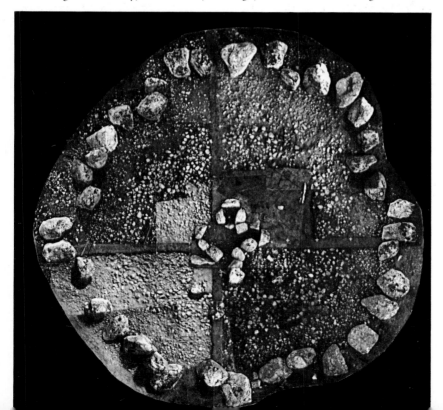

21 Antler pin fragment and walrus bone ring from Grave 27 at Carrowmore, Co. Sligo.

21 surface of the stone packing within the boulder circle produced rings of walrus bone, fragments of antler-pins (including one with a mushroom-shaped head), a stone bead, two balls of chalk, worked flint and some fragments of pottery resembling in its crude decoration, though technologically different in composition from, the Carrowkeel ware which is so typical of passage-tombs. Charcoal from the original megalithic construction produced closely clustered radiocarbon dates of $c.3090$, $c.3050$ and $c.2990$ bc. Although doubt has been cast on the relevance of these dates for assessing the period of building activity at Carrowmore, these dates are, nevertheless, among the earliest closely grouped dates available for any Irish megaliths. Because most of the dates available for other Irish megaliths are considerably younger, we must now proceed to re-examine the story of the various types of megalithic structures in the light of the recent evidence, though discussion of the wedge-tombs will be left until the next chapter.

## Court cairns

The first major type of megalithic monument to claim our attention here is the court cairn. In the past, it has variously been called court tomb, lobster-claw cairn, horned cairn and court grave. These names have all been used in order to emphasize one or more of its distinguishing features – a rounded forecourt leading to a flat-roofed gallery, standing at one (usually the eastern) end of a trapezoidal, ovoid or coffin-shaped mound. The façade of the forecourt can form more or less than a semicircle, and is made of upright stones which often have smaller, horizontally laid stones filling the gaps between them. The two central stones of this rough semicircle are often more marked than the others, as they stand guard at the entrance to the megalithic gallery behind them. This gallery is usually subdivided into two, three or sometimes even four, separate chambers, the division being created by upright jambs in the side-walls placed sufficiently far apart to allow access to the hindmost section. Where traces of the chamber roof have survived, they are large flat stones placed directly on the upright orthostats forming the walls of the chamber, though occasionally small corbel stones have been placed above them for the roof-stone to rest on. About thirty court cairns have one, or sometimes two, subsidiary chambers located in the hind-part of the cairn, with an entrance from the outside which is totally independent of the main megalithic gallery leading off the forecourt. A few of these side chambers retain traces of corbelling in the roof structure, but only in one case has a capstone survived. It is these subsidiary chambers which some people have claimed to be the ancestor of the portal-tomb in Ireland (see below).

One of the earliest court cairns to have been explored scientifically was that at Ballyalton, Co. Down, which was excavated by Estyn Evans and Oliver Davies in 1933. It is set in an egg-shaped mound 37 m by 21 m in maximum dimensions, the 'business end' being at the southwest. The forecourt façade was only slightly rounded and mildly asymmetrical, and the area in front of it was roughly paved. An unusual feature was the presence of an upright stone 80 cm high at the outermost point of the forecourt, which may have marked the boundary of the ritual area. In addition, there was a curious bank containing pottery sherds in the forecourt. Where one of the missing stones of the façade stood originally, there was a pit containing a ritual deposit of fourty-four flints and a spindle whorl, found at depths varying from 15 to 80 cm. The portal stones, lacking any surviving lintels, were about 50 cm lower than the other stones of the façade, and a minimum of 30 cm apart. They led into a group of conjoined chambers which, together, had a length of 10 m, and which were separated by jambs, though destruction made it difficult to know whether there had been two or three subdivisions in the gallery.

In the chambers a number of potsherds were found, including almost the whole of a decorated bowl of a type which has since been named after this site, and which the excavators claimed was the first 'Neolithic' vessel from Ireland to have been found in an organized excavation. Underneath this pot was a paving, below which was a black layer containing human and animal bones, teeth, broken pots, charcoal and worked flints. Within the cairn itself, to the southwest of the gallery, there was a stone-lined pit containing charcoal, burnt flint and about a dozen sherds, but its purpose remains obscure. Most of the pottery from the excavation was round-bottomed, shouldered ware of Sandhills type and of Ballymarlagh style, as well as the decorated pot of Ballyalton style, and other finds included hollow-based flint arrowheads. The bones found comprised the remains of at least seven individuals, some burned, others unburned, and the animals represented were sheep/goat, wolf or dog, cattle, pig and possibly deer. One interesting feature of this monument was the black layer

23  beneath the decorated pot. The court cairn at Browndod, Co. Antrim, proved to have had a similar layer though, in this instance, of bright red earth, which had been laid down extensively before the cairn was built.

These two examples, Ballyalton and Browndod, may be taken as representatives of the simplest, and what may also be the most basic, type of court cairn, as found in east Ulster. But more complicated variant forms are found both in Ulster and further westwards in north Connacht. One of these is the dual court cairn where, in plan, two such courts are placed at either end of a cairn, sometimes actually back to back – as at

23  Cohaw, Co. Cavan, or with a small space between them – as at Audleystown, Co. Down. Cohaw produced a Neolithic shouldered pot, the cremated bones of one or two children, and the skull of a youth. Audleystown, which unusually had the kerbstones of the cairn constructed of drystone walling, had corbel stones remaining above the orthostats of the chamber, suggesting that it may have been corbelled, rather than having been roofed by the more usual method of flat stones. The chambers, which were paved, had primary deposits consisting of stones and (again) black earth containing scattered human bones – some cremated (as is usual in court cairns), others unburnt – together with decorated and undecorated pottery sherds, lozenge-shaped flint arrowheads and hollow scrapers. Remains of no less than seventeen individuals were found in each of the chambers, suggesting to the excavator, Pat Collins, that all had been deposited in a fleshless state, and had therefore been stored elsewhere before their final interment.

Another significant variant of the court cairn ground-plan occurs mainly in Donegal and north Connacht. This is the central court cairn, in which the open court is contained within the trapezoidal mound, with covered galleries leading off one or both ends of the open court. One

22, 23  example, at Creevykeel, Co. Sligo, was fully excavated by the fourth Harvard Archaeological Mission to Ireland in 1935. It had a wedge-shaped mound, almost 70 m long, with an entrance to the court at the eastern end. The court itself measured about 17 m long and 10 m wide, and was originally paved with slabs or cobbles. Shallow pits in the gallery

22,23 **Court cairns** (*Above*) The central court cairn at Creevykeel, Co. Sligo.
(*Below*) Plans of court cairns, clockwise from above left: Browndod, Co. Antrim;
Cohaw, Co. Cavan; Treanmacmurtagh, Co. Sligo; and Creevykeel.

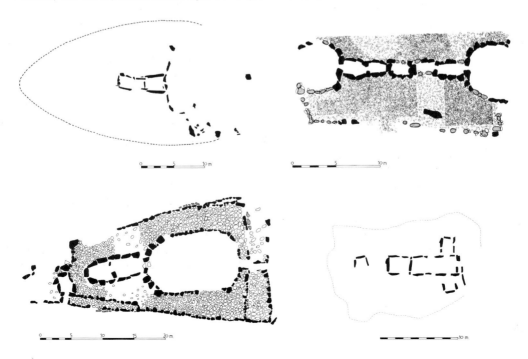

chambers contained four cremation burials, one accompanied by a flint hollow scraper. Other finds included shouldered Neolithic pottery, polished axes, a stone bead, leaf-shaped arrowheads and two clay balls of the kind more usually associated with passage-tombs.

About eight or nine court cairns in Sligo and Mayo have one characteristic which sets them apart from the others. This is the presence in the megalithic gallery of side chambers which, on plan, look like the transepts of a church, as at Treanmacmurtagh, Co. Sligo. Similar features are found in the long barrows of the Severn-Cotswold area of England as well as in southern Brittany, and efforts have been made to derive this transeptal feature in the court cairns from one or other of these areas. But, as Michael J. O'Kelly remarked, their existence in north Connacht may well be explained by the proximity to the Carrowkeel passage-tombs (of which more below), where this characteristic is also at home. One of these transeptal court cairns was that at Behy which is probably to be associated with the field fences and an oval Neolithic enclosure there. This court cairn, excavated by Ruaidhrí de Valera, Michael Herity and Seán Ó Nualláin in 1963 and 1964, was well preserved, as it was almost entirely overlain by bog which had grown up after it was built. The finds from Behy included plain, shouldered Neolithic pottery with out-turned flattened rims, a miniature stone axe, portions of two fine bifacially flaked laurel-leaf lance-heads of flint, and several hollow scrapers of chert.

About 38 out of the total of 329 court cairns have been excavated so far, and generally the finds recovered have been fairly uniform. The most typical pottery is the plain, round-bottomed 'Western Neolithic' ware of Case's Dunmurry, Ballymarlagh and Lyles Hill styles, as well as the more decorative Ballyalton and Goodland bowls. Sandhills ware also occurs, as does a coarser type of flat-bottomed pottery. Among the finds made of flint and chert, two types occur frequently – leaf-shaped arrowheads and hollow scrapers, though a slug knife also came to light at Creevykeel. The court cairn at Ballymacaldrack in Co. Antrim produced a porcellanite axe of Tievebulliagh type, while that at Clontygora in Co. Armagh contained an axe of epidiorite.

It is not at all clear whether the primary function of court cairns was that of a place of burial. Many of the excavated examples have produced comparatively little positive evidence for the primary – as opposed to secondary – burials of individuals, with the exception of places such as Audleystown (see above). In many cases, the excavated court cairns proved to have been disturbed or to contain material which was deposited secondarily. It is very rare that pottery was recovered in anything like an intact state, and sometimes sherds from the same pot were widely scattered within the chamber. One explanation for this is that the original burials may have been subsequently moved, but the reasonable hypothesis has also been put forward that court cairns were not primarily places for burials, but were 'temples' where the ritual involved would have taken place in the forecourt, and where the pottery-laden layers of black or red earth found in Ballyalton and Browndod, for instance, may have been gathered up from earlier remains on the site and deposited in the galleries or laid down before they were built, in order to create a sympathetic magic to ensure good harvests.

It is certainly noteworthy that court cairns are never grouped together as cemeteries, and in their isolation, they may have served as the focal cult centre for a scattered population, as the parish church does for the rural community of the Irish countryside today. They are located on average about 3 miles apart, and where they are closer together, they are never as near to one another as are some of the long barrows in the Severn-Cotswold region of southwestern England.

Gabriel Cooney's examination of the megaliths in Co. Leitrim showed that the court cairns tended to hug the rocky upland areas, where light and well-drained soils provided suitable terrain for early farmers. The houses of the builders of court cairns have yet to be located, but the case of Behy quoted above suggests that the settlements of the living and the court cairns were not far apart, and seemed to have formed a unit. Court cairns give the impression of being the product of an egalitarian society, broken down into individual local and domestic groupings of perhaps no more than 50–100 people, who were using the cairns to establish their ancestral rights over the minimum amount of land they needed to survive. The likelihood is that their builders lived in comparative political and economic isolation, largely unaffected by any bonus benefit which may have accrued from items such as the Tievebulliagh or Rathlin Island axe trade, which may have been exploited by only a few.

The vast majority of court cairns lie north of a line from Galway to Dundalk and, as we have seen, the dual court cairns tend to cluster in south Ulster, while the central court cairns are largely confined to Donegal, Sligo and Mayo. The concentration of court cairns in north Connacht, and particularly in Mayo, has led De Valera and others to the view that it was in this area that the court cairns developed, with the gradual reduction in size and features further east, suggesting an eastward movement across Ulster and thence into Scotland, where similar tombs are known in the Clyde area. But the single radiocarbon determination relevant to the Mayo tombs, for what it is worth, does not necessarily support the theory. This is the date of $c.2730$ bc for the house at Ballyglass, Co. Mayo, which almost certainly preceded the building of the court cairn there, but probably not by any great length of time.

In contrast, the court cairns of Ulster have produced earlier dates. The court cairn which Dudley Waterman carefully uncovered in 1976 at Tully, Co. Fermanagh, produced dates ranging from $c.3010–c.2495$ bc, leading Waterman to suggest that it had been constructed in the earlier part of the third millennium bc. Charcoal associated with Neolithic pottery in the dual court cairn at Carnanbane, Co. Tyrone, gave dates of *c*.3095 and *c*.2980 bc, which are sufficiently close to those at Tully to suggest that the earliest date of all for a court cairn, that of *c*.4975 bc for Ballymacdermot, Co. Armagh (which also gave another radiocarbon reading stretching into the Christian era), may be too far outside the general 'run' of dates to be taken as anything but anomalous.

The other important court cairn from the point of view of radiocarbon dating is Dooey's Cairn at Ballymacaldrack, Co. Antrim. Here, the forecourt had one megalithic chamber leading off it, beyond which was a so-called 'cremation passage' with walls not of megalithic construction, but of simple boulders piled up one on top of the other. Charcoal from the inner end of the 'cremation passage' produced a date of *c*.2990 bc, and another sample from wall crevices worked out at *c*.3200 bc. But as the forecourt blocking the court cairn itself gave a date of *c*.2680 bc, it seems as if the 'cremation passage' was 500 years older than the construction of the court cairn.

Further dates for court cairns, such as Ballyutoag, Co. Antrim (*c*.2170 bc), bring us well into the second half of the third millennium bc. The earliest dates recovered so far would suggest that the first Ulster court cairns were probably earlier than the first Connacht court cairns, though a single date from the latter province is obviously an insufficient sample on which to base any firm conclusion. The concentration in Connacht could be accounted for by the notion suggested by Pat Collins that, as the court cairn builders coming from Ulster could go no further westwards, they stayed there and continued to build court cairns for a long time.

But even if Irish court cairns were first built in Ulster, their ultimate origin still remains a problem. Despite the similarities between the handful of transeptal cairns in Mayo and Sligo to the Severn-Cotswold and Breton tombs, an origin for the basic design of the Irish court cairn is more likely to be sought in Scotland than anywhere else, as similar cairns have been found there. We do not have to envisage the arrival from overseas of hordes of megalith builders to explain the presence of so many court cairns, in the same way that it is not necessary to conjure up an army of French and English clerics and masons to explain the advent of Romanesque churches in Ireland thousands of years later. All you need is a few people to introduce the idea, and court cairns could still be explained as the adaptation of a general Western European idea by an otherwise indigenous population consisting not of the earliest farmers, as De Valera thought, but of an amalgam of Mesolithic hunters and Neolithic farmers which resulted from twenty generations or more of intermarriage.

## Portal-tombs

Portal-tombs or -chambers, otherwise known as portal dolmens or graves, are the simplest but also the most dramatic of all the Irish megalithic monuments, particularly when viewed against the skyline. Many have a grace and poise which foreshadows some of the best of modern sculpture.

24 Portal-tomb at Kilclooney, Co. Donegal.

One at Kilclooney, Co. Donegal, bears an elegant resemblance to a bird    24
about to take flight, and you could be forgiven for seeing in it the original
design for the Concorde aeroplane!

   Portal-tombs are above-ground burial chambers, consisting of between three and seven uprights carrying one or two very heavy capstones
which slope downwards towards the back. The example from Legananny,    25
Co. Down, could easily be mistaken for a three-legged table at a giant's
tea-party. Indeed, the old word dolmen, formerly used to describe such
tombs, comes itself from two Breton words meaning 'stone table'. Less
than 200 years ago, our ancestors presumed them to have been druids'
altars. But excavations in a few of the 161 known examples have produced
cremated bone, or a combination of cremation and inhumation, so that it
is now generally accepted that they were used for burial purposes. To help
seal the chamber, smaller stones were sometimes inserted between the
uprights, and the space between the two large portal stones forming the
entrance may have been fully or partially blocked by an extra stone. On
occasions, the portal stones had a further stone flanking them externally,
almost giving the impression that there was a small forecourt in front of
the tomb entrance.

About twenty-five portal-tombs show traces of having stood in a long mound. The unique mound at Malin More in Co. Donegal had one large chamber at either end, and in the 90 m which separated them, four separate smaller chambers were located, placed at right angles to the mound. Despite occasional suggestions to the contrary, there is no compelling reason to believe that the round mounds completely covered the portal-tombs, and the visually impressive form of the portal-tombs is a contributory reason for thinking that they were originally planned as free-standing monuments. Nevertheless, the mound at the back of the tomb may once have been higher than it stands today, as the massive capstone was presumably placed in position on top of the upright stones by being hauled or heaved up an earthen ramp from behind, probably by means of rollers made of tree-stems.

The siting of portal-tombs has a tendency to cling to river valleys, often at an altitude of between 100 m and 300 m, and almost half of the examples known are located within about 5 miles of the coast. The distribution of these tombs is concentrated in the north and northwest of the country, though with a significant spread in a line from Dublin to Waterford. Their northern distribution tallies reasonably well with that of court cairns, and as their form resembles some of the separate chambers in the sides of the court cairn mounds, it has been suggested that – like Eve being created out of one of Adam's ribs – portal-tombs developed from court cairns in mid- to west-Ulster, spreading from there southwards into Leinster and from thence across the Irish Sea to Wales and Cornwall. Certainly, the flint hollow scrapers, the 'Western Neolithic' and ornamental wares such as that found at Ballykeel, Co. Armagh, correspond fairly closely to the finds from court cairns. Yet the case for deriving portal-tombs from court cairns is far from proven, for the radiocarbon 26 date of $c$.3290 bc for the polygonal chamber at Carrowmore (Grave 7) mentioned above is earlier than any date for a court cairn, with the exception of the probably aberrant date of $c$.4975 bc for Ballymacdermot, Co. Armagh. In both of these cases, we can apply the recent adage that one radiocarbon date is no radiocarbon date, as one needs several to cross-check, and the uncertainty of the relationship between the Carrowmore chamber and the specimen material from which the radiocarbon date was obtained, would make it unwise to claim that the Grave 7 chamber at Carrowmore is the ancestor of the Irish portal-tomb. Nevertheless, the Carrowmore evidence must also make us wary of over-reliance on the theory that portal-tombs grew out of court cairns, and the possibility must be borne in mind that these portal-tombs – in their very simplicity – could have been one of the earliest types of megalithic monument in Ireland. Their important emphasis on coastal distribution, instanced by the case of the Malin More tombs which are cut off by hills from the surrounding land-mass, could lead to the notion that their builders arrived separately by sea, or that they were largely coastal dwellers with connections across

25 Portal-tomb at Legananny, Co. Down. ▷

the sea who shared common pottery and artefacts with the court cairn builders further inland. The derivation of portal-tombs from the side-chambers of court cairns is not the only possible interpretation for their similarity, for the court cairn builders could also be seen as accommodating in their monuments the separate ritual requirements for a particular part of the population which would otherwise have used the portal-tombs. But, with the lack of any further reliable evidence, the question of the origin of the Irish portal dolmen must remain an enigma.

Perhaps further radiocarbon dates may help to justify or repudiate the theory that portal-tombs spread from western and central Ulster down into Leinster, despite the considerable geographical gap between the two groups. Rather than becoming a part of dogma, the possibility of an Irish origin for Welsh and Cornish tombs of the same kind must also remain an open question, as portal-tombs occur in a number of variants on the European Continent. We should not forget that one portal-tomb in Wales – Dyffryn Ardudwy – produced pottery looking as early as any Neolithic pottery in the 'British Isles'. This, at any rate, was the judgment of its excavator, Terence Powell, who also examined an Irish megalith at Ballynamona Lower in Co. Waterford, which could be classified either as a court cairn or a portal-tomb. But its pottery considerably resembles that from single burials which, as we shall see below, are now firmly datable to the first half of the third millennium bc, rather than to the Late Neolithic as heretofore. The argument for seeing portal-tombs as being contemporary with the later stages of court cairn construction, and therefore with the Late Neolithic, ought to be deleted from the record, leaving the way open for a much earlier beginning for the portal-tombs in Ireland; yet while the radiocarbon date of c.1400 bc for the example at Ballykeel in Co. Armagh is regarded as 'anomalous', it must nevertheless make us aware of the possibility that portal-tombs may have had a long and useful life in this country.

### The great passage-tombs

Together with the temples of Malta, passage-tombs are the first great achievements of monumental architecture anywhere in prehistoric Europe, and – in the Boyne Valley – Ireland can claim to have some of the most remarkable of them.

As their name suggests, they are graves in which access to a burial chamber is gained through a passage, both of which are covered by a round mound of earth and stone. In an obvious display of importance, the passage-tombs are often on the tops of hills or ridges, where they could be seen for miles around. The concept of the passage-tomb – an above-ground passage and chamber covered by a man-made mound – is one found in a different form in the pyramids of Egypt, and also in the great tombs of Mycenae, but any connection with them has been shown to be nebulous by the earlier radiocarbon dating of the passage-tombs. In fact,

26 Carrowmore, Co. Sligo: Grave 7 in the foreground, with Queen Maeve's grave on Knocknarea visible in the far distance.

the passage-tomb is largely a West European phenomenon, being found mainly in the countries bordering the Atlantic littoral – Spain, Portugal, France, Ireland, Wales, Scotland and Scandinavia.

The Irish passage-tombs are often grouped together in major cemeteries such as those in the Boyne Valley, including Newgrange, Knowth and Dowth, and Loughcrew – all in Co. Meath – and Carrowmore and Carrowkeel, both in Co. Sligo. In many instances, we often find one outstandingly large passage-tomb, around which smaller 'satellite' tombs seem to cluster, like chicks around the mother hen. The two Sligo cemeteries of Carrowmore and Carrowkeel have the major tomb on a hill some considerable distance away, namely Queen Maeve's grave on Knocknarea, and Keshcorran respectively. Indeed, Queen Maeve's 26 grave of Knocknarea, west of Sligo town, is not only one of the largest passage-tombs known, but it is also one of the unforgettable reminiscences of Stone Age vision when seen from the Carrowmore cemetery below it.

These major cemeteries indicate the main distribution of passage-tombs stretching across the north midlands from the mouth of the Boyne to Sligo Bay. But there are other important passage-tombs, often more isolated, in various parts of Ulster and on hill-tops in south Leinster, such as Seefin, though there are very few in Munster.

Over this considerable range of territory, the passage-tombs show a fairly uniform burial rite and assemblage of gravegoods. In almost all cases where such tombs have been excavated, they have produced cremation burials, with inhumation being generally rarer. Obviously when only small fragments of cremated bone remain, it is difficult to estimate accurately the actual numbers of individuals buried in any one tomb. But at Fourknocks in Co. Meath, Patrick Hartnett was able to show that the tomb was the final resting place for the cremated and inhumed remains of over sixty people. It has been suggested that there may have been more than 100 individuals buried in the Mound of the Hostages on the Hill of Tara in Co. Meath, but we still await the publication of the excavation report to know how many of these may belong to a later period. These tombs were, therefore, unlike the pyramids, communal graves which may well have been used for several generations, like the family vaults of today. At Fourknocks, 28 adults and 3 children had been cremated, but only 16 adults inhumed. The adults ranged in age from twenty-five to fifty years, and where it proved possible to determine the sexes, it emerged that there were 3 males and 1 female. The remains of 20 cremated individuals were found in the eastern tomb at Knowth, while in the great burial chamber at Newgrange, the number may have been no more than 6. We may think of passage-tombs as having been the burial places of outstanding chieftains, or, alternatively, we may consider them as being the final resting places of one or of a few families over a number of generations. But the small crumbs of cremated bone found prevent us from knowing whether the dead belonged to one or more families.

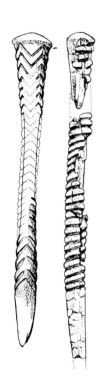

27 Bone pin from Fourknocks with herring-bone decoration (left) and a comparable grooved example (right) from Knowth.

The pottery typical of the passage-tombs is Carrowkeel ware. This cf. ▮ somewhat roughly textured pottery, often with coarse decoration, stands in contrast to the finely executed ornament on the stones of some of the passage-tombs in the eastern part of the country. Bone was a material beloved of passage-tomb builders, and they used it for making a variety of pins, some mushroom-headed, which have come to light in the excavated graves. One of the pins recovered at Fourknocks bears geometrical herring-bone decoration, and another from Knowth is grooved. Precisely what the purpose of these pins was, we cannot say. The oft-repeated explanation that they may have served to hold together a leather bag in which the cremated remains of the dead were laid in the tomb is rendered improbable by the fact that many of them seem to bear traces of fire – probably that of the funeral pyre. They may, therefore, have been used to fasten cloaks.

Small stone pendants were frequently found in passage-tombs, and they presumably represented personal ornaments worn by those buried, though they may also have served as a talisman. One of the most popular shapes was that of a miniature pestle- or hammer-head, though a few examples look more like an axe. The stone used was often soapstone or limestone, though some were made of finer material such as jasper or carnelian. A number of small beads of the same materials may also be counted among the ornaments of the passage-tomb builders. One of the more enigmatic types of object found were the balls of stone, or, quite frequently, of chalk, which occasionally reached the size of a tennis ball. What their purpose was, we know not, but a sexual connotation – like the phallic significance put forward for the mushroom-headed bone pins – would appear to be somewhat dubious. Of more likely sexual significance are the small round-headed stones known as baetyls found outside the Knowth mound. Unusually for the Stone Age, flint is rarely found among the passage-tombs, though one of the most exotic objects of all from any tomb is the macehead from Knowth (see below), which is made of this material.

The excavation at Carrowmore, particularly of Grave 27, produced    20 material which seems to fit best that which is known from passage-tombs, and the fact that the rounded kerb is the form found at Carrowmore only helps to strengthen the notion that this site ought to be regarded as a cemetery associated with those who built passage-tombs in other parts of Ireland. Different kinds of monument are represented there: portal-tombs with or without a surrounding circle of stones; and stone circles without any visible stone chamber inside. Even if we leave aside the somewhat disputed evidence of Grave 7 (which ought to warn us against    26 linking portal-tombs too closely with court cairns), Grave 27, recently excavated by Burenhult, shows us that a type of cruciform tomb within a circular kerb of stones, and with gravegoods of the kind found in passage-tombs, was already in existence apparently in the late fourth millennium bc. The tomb could be said to conform to the normal passage-tomb type – except for the paradoxical fact that it does not have a passage! But this need not deter us from presuming that the same people who were to build passage-tombs proper in Co. Sligo and other parts of Ireland were building megalithic tombs without passages at Carrowmore in the fourth millennium bc. As the dates provided for Grave 27 (*c*.3090–*c*.2990 bc) are considered, at least by some, to be the earliest for any monument belonging to the passage-tomb tradition in Ireland, we may reasonably presume that Grave 27 at Carrowmore represents some form of early version of a passage-tomb, before the passage itself became the standard form, and possibly before collective burial practised over several generations became the norm. On the evidence of the radiocarbon dates, the ensuing 1,000 years was to see the building of many passage-tombs in Ireland.

As we shall see below, the radiocarbon dates for the fully developed passage-tombs are some centuries later than those for Grave 27 at Carrowmore. This could theoretically be interpreted as suggesting that the earliest passage-tombs were built in the west, particularly in Co. Sligo, and that the people who built them moved (or passed on the idea) eastwards, where some of the great passage-tombs were built in the Boyne

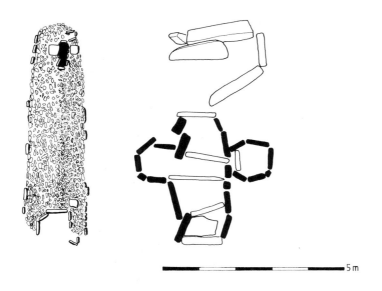

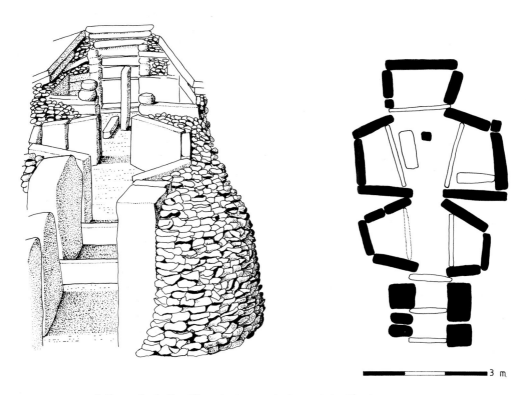

28 Carrowkeel, Co. Sligo: (*top*) general plan and detail (with 5-m scale) of Cairn E; (*above*) reconstruction and plan of Cairn F.

Valley. But while it now transpires that these great passage-tombs in Co. Meath are not the beginning but the zenith of passage-tomb building in Ireland, the few radiocarbon dates that we have must make us cautious about presuming that those in the west are the earliest, for other even earlier dates may yet come from examples to be excavated elsewhere in the future. The possibility must also be kept in mind that passage-tombs in the east and west of the country, characterized among other things by the presence or absence of decorated stones, may represent two independent or semi-independent foci of development. One way or another, it is clear that passage-tombs were built over many centuries in various parts of Ireland, and it is to those examples outside Carrowmore that we must now turn.

In the same county of Sligo is the cemetery on a limestone plateau at Carrowkeel, in a very dramatic setting overlooking Lough Arrow. It consists of more than a dozen passage-tombs and allied structures, almost all in round stone mounds, and covered by a later layer of peat which had helped to preserve them until they were rather summarily excavated in 1911. The 'classic' form consisted of a passage and a burial chamber off which lay three burial niches, placed in such a way as to give the whole a cruciform plan. The walls were made of large stones, and the roof was corbelled in very fine masonry. Cairn F, one of the best constructed of all,    28 had a second set of burial niches on the side. One of the most enigmatic monuments in the cemetery is Cairn E which – unlike the others – was placed in a long mound. It had a blind façade forming a sort of forecourt, like those of the court cairns, at one end, and a small passage-tomb at the other end. Yet its contents did not differ markedly from those of the other graves in the cemetery, which conformed to the typical passage-tomb assemblage. Cairn H had a passage and a chamber which were scarcely differentiated from one another – a kind which we shall have reason to refer to again. There were also a few monuments which, like Grave 27 at Carrowmore, had no passage leading to them.

Carrowkeel was excavated, if such is the term, before the discovery of the use of the radiocarbon method, and we have, therefore, no way of dating the cemetery relative to others of the same kind. Playing with the hypothetical development of ground-plans, without having a secure start or finish, is a pointless exercise, and we must await further excavation of a more careful nature before we can find out where Carrowkeel fits into the overall chronological picture. Seventy years further research since the original excavations at Carrowkeel have, however, now shown that the tombs date to the Stone, not the Bronze Age, as the excavators had originally thought on the basis of the pottery alone, the lack of bronze being, in their view, because it was too valuable a material to waste on tomb deposits.

An even cruder and sadder case of rifling before the advent of scientific excavation is the case of the great passage-tomb cemetery about 50 miles

29,30 **The Loughcrew passage tombs, Co. Meath** (*Opposite*) Aerial view of Carnbane West; the large tomb in the foreground is Cairn L. (*Above*) View of Cairn S.

eastwards at Loughcrew, otherwise known as *Sliabh na Caillighe* (The Hill of the Witch), near Oldcastle in the northwestern corner of the pasture-rich county of Meath. Here, the passage-tombs sited on a series of hill-tops had been 'excavated' in the last century, without – unlike Carrowkeel – any proper records being kept of the plunderings. Yet what did emerge conformed to the pottery and bonework of the passage-tomb peoples, with the exception of some decorated Iron Age bone fragments found in one of the tombs.

The same sense of dramatic siting can be felt about these tombs, which must number over thirty. They vary considerably in size, the largest mound having a diameter of 55 m, and usually each hill-top has one tomb which is larger than the others clustering close to it. The tomb-plans bear a considerable resemblance to those at Carrowkeel, with the passage leading to cruciform burial chambers, or to those which have two 'stalls' or burial niches placed next to one another on each side. The Y-shaped tomb in Cairn S is unique in plan. One feature found at Loughcrew, though absent in Sligo, is the presence of a large stone basin of uncertain, though probably ritual, use inside the tomb. But another, potentially

29

30

31,32 **Decorated stones in Co. Meath** (*Opposite*) Interior of Cairn T at Loughcrew, showing the heavily ornamented stone at the rear of the chamber. (*Above*) Selection of motifs used on decorated stones of the passage tombs in Co. Meath.

more significant difference between the Sligo and Loughcrew tombs, is the existence of decoration, or 'art', on many of the stones of the Meath necropolis. This art has been applied by the pocking technique, and consists of a variety of geometrical motifs: circles, U-shaped arcs, parallel lines, radial sun-like patterns, snake-like shapes, zigzags, ovals, spirals and a so-called off-set motif. In addition, lozenges, triangles and chevrons make brief appearances, and cupmarks and dots are quite common. A number of these motifs occur on other Irish passage-tombs in the eastern half of the country, of which the most remarkable are found in the same county of Meath, and particularly in the Boyne Valley.

31, 32

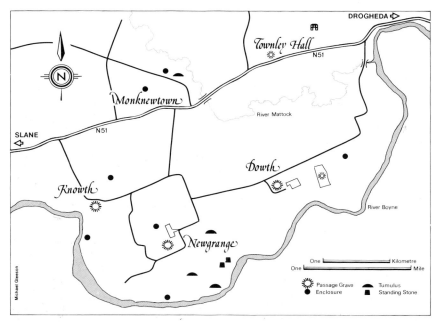

33 The main monuments in the Boyne Valley, Co. Meath.

Unlike Carrowkeel and Loughcrew, the Boyne Valley tombs have the inestimable advantage that some of them have been the subject of the most detailed and careful modern excavation, which has also produced a limited but nevertheless significant number of radiocarbon dates. The three famous tombs which make up a major cemetery of passage-tombs 33 are Newgrange, Knowth and Dowth. Dowth is a large mound 85 m in diameter and originally about 16 m high, though it has been much disfigured in the burrowings which took place from the top downwards in 1847–48. Two different-sized passage-tombs are present in the south-western sector of the mound, one cruciform in plan with an inward extension of the southern niche, and the other having a round chamber with one burial niche leading off to the right as you enter. These tombs occupy such a small part of the whole mound that one might well ask if a further tomb or tombs still remain to be discovered within it. The finds from the 'excavations' in the last century were insignificant, and largely of much later date, but some of the kerbstones of the mound bear interesting decoration, including the rayed motif already encountered at Loughcrew.

George Eogan's excavations conducted annually since 1962 have shown Knowth to be a much more exciting monument. It is somewhat larger than Dowth, having an almost oval mound varying in diameter from 80 to 95 m, 9.9 m high and covering more than 0.4 hectares (1½ acres). The mound is made up of sods, clay, stones and shale, layered one above

34 Cross-section of Site 1 at Knowth, displaying the varied layers that make up the mound's structure.

the other rather like a chocolate cake. This large mound, known as Site 1,   34
makes use of a considerable number of large stones, up to 4 tons in weight,
many of which were probably quarried in the locality within a distance of
5–8 miles, though some other smaller stones may have been brought to the
site from the Dundalk or Newry area, some 40 km away. Around the large
mound there are eighteen smaller, and often partially dilapidated, round
mounds containing tombs with varying ground-plans, and known as

satellite tombs. One of these, Site 16, proved to be earlier than the large tomb, as the kerb of the large mound changed its course to avoid the smaller example, which has a burial chamber only marginally larger than its passage. Site 16 demonstrates that the earliest type of tomb-plan at Knowth was that with an undifferentiated passage and chamber, though the type continued to be used subsequently side-by-side with other less numerous tombs with a ground-plan in the shape of a cross. The radio-carbon determination for Site 16 was *c*.2449 bc, which is marginally later than those of *c*.2540 and *c*.2455 bc for the building of the main mound, and the date of *c*.2795 for the redeposited turves at its base. While this would at first sight seem to conflict with the archaeological evidence for the satellite tomb 16 being earlier than the main mound, the permissible range of error in these dates still allows for the prior construction of Site 16, but suggests that the interval between the building of the two is unlikely to have been more than a few decades at most. Finds from beneath some of the satellite tombs indicated activity, domestic or otherwise, on the site before the tombs were built. Site 13 was another satellite tomb apparently built before the main mound, and the fact that both it and Site 16 had their tombs orientated towards where the large mound now stands suggests that the large mound covers an area where some burial or ritual may have taken place before the vast mound was heaped over it.

35, 36     The main feature at Knowth is undoubtedly the large mound, Site 1, which has produced a number of astounding surprises during the course of the excavations. The first of these was that the large round mound contained not one but two great passage-tombs, which were built almost back to back at the same time. They are orientated towards the east and west respectively, and George Eogan has recently suggested that they may be purposely orientated towards where the sun rose on 20 or 21 March and set on 22 or 23 September, an equinoctial orientation which could associate them with the marking of the sowing season and the gathering in of the harvest.

Both of the tombs have similar incurving entrances, but they differ radically in plan in that they each represent one of the main types of tomb-plan in the satellite tombs outside them, the undifferentiated and the cruciform, thus forming an intentional symbiosis of the two. The western tomb measures 34.2 m in length, and is of the undifferentiated variety, though it is not absolutely straight, as there is an 'elbow' about three-quarters of the way along its length, where the passage turns slightly to the right. Further along there is a sill-stone, formally dividing passage from chamber, which is little more than a widening of the passage, though

35,36 (*Opposite*) **Knowth in overview** (*Above*) Glimpse from the air, with the grid squares of the excavation prominently displayed, and the entrance to the western passage-tomb visible at the left of the main mound. (*Below*) Plan of the main mound and its satellites.

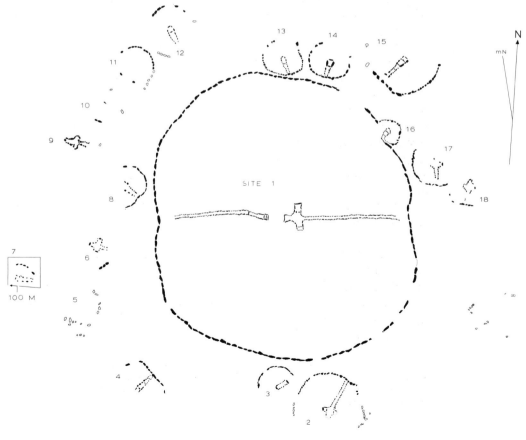

N

mN

13  14  15

12

11

10

9

SITE 1

16

17

8

18

7

6

100 M

5

4

3

2

50 Metres    50 Yards

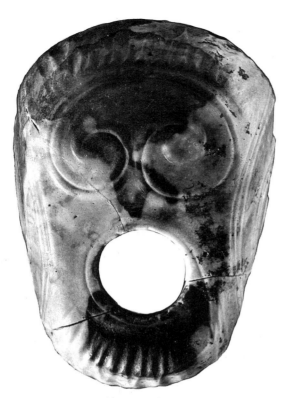

37,38 **The Knowth macehead** (*Left* and
*opposite*) Photograph and roll-out drawing of
this remarkable ceremonial flint macehead,
7.9 cm long, discovered in one of the recesses
of the eastern tomb chamber. It would
originally have been mounted on a wooden
handle through the large hole.

slightly taller than it. Both passage and chamber are roofed with large, flat
stones. At the elbow, there is a large stone basin which was almost
certainly dragged to its present position from nearer the back of the tomb.
The tomb itself has not yet been excavated, but flakes of cremated bone
are already visible in the fill of soft earth over the floor of the chamber, and
the same area has yielded part of a stone pestle or mace-head, and part of
the stem of a large antler-pin.

The eastern tomb, entered at almost the diagonally opposite point in
the mound, totals 40.4 m in length, making it probably the longest
passage-tomb in the whole of Atlantic Europe. But, unlike the western
tomb, the passage broadens out here into a cruciform chamber, with a
burial niche on either side, and a third at the back. The roof of the
chamber rises to a height of 5.9 m, and is built on the corbel principle, that
is, the large stones are placed one on top of the other in ever-decreasing
circles until the gap can be closed by a single stone. The right-hand niche
is the largest of the three, and resting inside it is a richly decorated stone
39    basin, its front ornamented with concentric circles on which a number of
horizontal lines converge, and its concave upper surface bearing grooves
of radial and concentric circular lines. Most of the evidence for burials in
this eastern chamber came from the largely cremated bone fragments in
the three tomb-recesses, which spilled over into the central point of the
cruciform chamber. The burials were mainly concentrated in the left-
hand recess, surrounding an empty central area where a stone basin found

`|——————————————|` 5 cm

39 Decorated stone basin in the right-hand recess of the eastern tomb at Knowth.

40 Stone with decoration looking like a stylized human face in the western tomb at Knowth.

37, 38 in a disturbed layer above it had presumably lain originally. Near the entrance to this tomb was found the very exotic flint macehead which is decorated with sunken lozenge-shaped facets and superbly executed spirals, some of which, when taken together with the shaft-hole, give the impression of representing a human face. Other finds included pestle-pendants and mushroom-headed and other pin fragments. Part of a flint macehead was also found nearby.

Other than the discovery of two major tombs back to back under the same mound, the greatest surprise of the Knowth excavations has been the uncovering of a considerable number of decorated stones, which have added greatly to the repertoire of passage-tomb art, and which have virtually doubled the number of decorated stones known from Irish passage-tombs. Both tombs have their walls heavily ornamented with various designs, usually executed in the pocking or incised technique. Many of these are purely abstract geometrical designs. But one, in the passage approaching the burial chamber in the western tomb, has what look like two eyes on top, so that the whole stone may be a very stylized version of the human figure.

40

The stones forming the kerb of the large mound are also richly decorated. On the whole, spirals, circles, arcs and serpentiform motifs predominate, without forming any coherent grouping. But two stones stand out from all the others. The one at the entrance to the western tomb   41 has a series of boxed rectangles, cut in the centre by a vertical groove, marking the axis or entrance to the tomb. Another stone on the southern side has what looks like the radiating lines of a sundial at the bottom centre, and a spiral at one side. The upper central part of the stone has been pocked, but is otherwise left undecorated, except for a central perforation.

The third of the great passage-tombs on the ridge of hills on the northern side of the Boyne is Newgrange which, in early Irish mythology,   44-47 played an important role not only as the alleged burial place of the prehistoric kings of Tara, but also as the home of that otherworld race of Irish supernatural beings, the *Tuatha de Danainn*, 'the people of the goddess Danu'. The latter were considered to have gone 'underground', but to have continued to live, nevertheless, performing supernatural deeds beyond the powers of ordinary mortals. Newgrange was also taken to be the house of the Dagda, the good god, whose son Oengus persuaded his father to give him the Brú (as the abode was known) for a day and a night. But when a day and a night had passed, Oengus explained that as today and tomorrow meant forever, he should retain the mound in perpetuity. Even today, Newgrange retains a never-ending fascination for its multitudinous visitors, providing them with ample material for wonderment, thought and theories, some more fanciful than others!

The great mound of Newgrange is built atop a small hillock, in a   44 dominant position overlooking the Boyne, that rich river which has   33 attracted invader and tourist down the centuries. Its female deity, Boand, also seems to be inextricably linked with the mythological history of the *Brú na Bóinne*. As at Knowth, Newgrange has its small satellite tombs, though very much fewer in number, only four being known so far. One of these, Site K, was an undifferentiated passage-tomb with a triangular-shaped annexe added to it subsequently, while another – Site L – had a cruciform plan, which had Neolithic settlement remains beneath it, as was also the case at Townleyhall and Knowth. A third site, undifferentiated in plan but with one side-chamber, had a basin-stone, as at Knowth.

But it is on the main mound that almost all the attention has been lavished since the tomb was discovered accidentally by the removal of material for road-metalling in 1699. The great mound is kidney-shaped,   49 measuring on average 103.6 m in diameter and over 13 m high. It has one passage-tomb where the mound curves inwards on its southeastern side. This passage follows the natural incline by rising about 2 m between the   48 entrance and the hindmost part of the burial chamber – a distance of 24.2 m, which makes it considerably shorter than either of the Knowth tombs. The innermost part of the tomb can be seen to reach almost, but

41–43 **Decorated stones** (*Above*) Kerbstone with a vertical groove marking the entrance to the western tomb at Knowth. (*Opposite, above*) The famous entrance stone at Newgrange, with a similar vertical groove. Behind it lies the opening to the

not quite, to the centre of the mound, and the presence of the two tombs back to back at Knowth poses the tantalizing question as to whether there may be a second great tomb under the Newgrange mound. Its dedicated excavator, Michael O'Kelly, who worked annually on the mound from 1962 until 1975, searched diligently but in vain for traces of a second chamber, though it may be there somewhere in the unexcavated half of the mound (perhaps at right angles to the one already known?).

However, he did uncover a great deal of information in and around the chamber area, when work was started at the behest of the Irish Tourist Board's archaeologist, Patrick Hartnett, in order to make the tomb safe for visitors. He found the remains of two inhumed individuals in the chamber, whose bones were scattered in various parts of the tomb, suggesting that they may have been buried there only secondarily. There were also the cremated remains of three or more people. Other finds included seven 'marbles', four pendants, two beads, a flint flake, a bone chisel and fragments of several bone pins and points – which could be considered to be a meagre harvest for such a large tomb, but it is surprising that even as much as that had survived in a tomb which had

passage, with the roof-box above. The smaller stones are a modern reconstruction.
(*Below*) Kerbstone 52 at Newgrange, which stands on the exactly opposite side of the
mound from the tomb entrance.

been open and visited by thousands of people since 1699. Certainly, what was found fitted well into the normal categories of finds from passage-tombs. Radiocarbon dates of *c*.2475 and *c*.2465 bc from soil between the roof-slabs of the passage suggested a date roughly contemporary with or only marginally later than the building of Knowth.

48  The tomb itself, which was built as an independent structure before it was covered by the mound, has the typical cross-shaped plan already encountered elsewhere, but – as in other examples too – the right-hand
47  niche is seen here to have been the most important, as its roofstone bears the most elaborate decoration of all the stones within the chamber. The roof is not so much corbelled, as in the eastern tomb at Knowth, but rather
46  built up on the beam-wall principle, which differs from the corbel system in that each stone does not lie on a single stone beneath it, but rather on the neighbouring halves of two adjoining stones below. This technique, which creates an interesting angular impression on the eye, is one which may have been borrowed from the woodworker. Each of the tomb-niches had a stone basin, none so beautifully decorated as the one from Knowth mentioned above, though that in the right-hand burial niche – the only one to survive intact – has two circular dells, of unknown use, in its concave upper surface. The stones of the roof of the chamber are not horizontal, but slope slightly downwards away from the centre, doubtless as a precaution to prevent damp percolating from above down into the chamber – the dryness of which to the present day is a remarkable testimony to the engineering skills of the builders. When he examined the upper surfaces of the passage and chamber stones, Michael O'Kelly found a number of grooves which also served apparently to drain off the rain-water – another clever touch.

A further interesting aspect of Newgrange – and the one which has made it internationally known in recent years – is the purposeful orientation of the central line of the passage to a point on the horizon where the sun rises on the shortest day of the year – the winter solstice of 21 December. When the orb of the sun climbs over the horizon on that day, its rays go straight through the doorway of the tomb, but because the passage behind the entrance rises gently upwards towards the burial chamber, those rays which come through the door only shine in about half
45  way along the upward-sloping passage. Because of this, the builders
42, 48  constructed a so-called 'roof-box' – a small opening above the doorway which allowed the sun's rays to enter horizontally at a sufficiently high level for them to penetrate along the whole length of the passage as far as the centre of the chamber, as O'Kelly discovered in 1968, though others had apparently suggested this possibility earlier. When he entered the chamber on midwinter-day of that year, he found that a pencil-thin ray of sunlight penetrated the chamber for a mere seventeen minutes, from 8.58 to 9.15 am winter time. While it also does so on a few days either side of the winter solstice, it otherwise disappears from the chamber for another

year. Those who visited the tomb by candlelight, in the days before electric light was installed, were able to experience some of the wonderment which the builders, and possibly some of their descendants, must have felt as they stood inside the chamber on midwinter's day, seeing the sun's rays making their fleeting annual appearance, and disappearing as quietly and as stealthily as they had come.

But what did the builders experience on the completion of the tomb? Other than at times of burial, did the living only visit the tomb at midwinter, pulling back the large stone which acted as a door at the entrance and which stands beside it still to this day, before entering the chamber where the dead were housed? We really cannot say. But the whole process of the sun's rays shining into the central chamber would seem to make most sense if interpreted as a sign as much for the living as for the dead, as would also seem to be the case at Knowth where the orientation may have been related to the planting and reaping of the crops to keep the living in food. In the same way that winter not only denotes the end of one of nature's annual cycles but also the dawn of a new one as well, so too the penetration of the sun's rays into the tomb could be taken to be symbolic of the end of mortal life for those buried within, yet also of the promise of a new life in the Otherworld – a sort of spiritual 'if winter comes, can spring be far behind?' The total contrast between the massive and monumental nature of this house for the dead, which is the Newgrange mound, and the huts of the builders so flimsy and ephemeral as not to have left a single trace behind them, shows how important the afterlife must have been for those who erected Newgrange, piling up perhaps a million sackfuls of earth and stone over a period variously estimated at between five and thirty years. It is only such a strong faith in a life in the world to come which can have helped to inspire the people into such a gigantic effort, one which has been rightly compared to the community effort involved in the building of a great cathedral in the Middle Ages, or the achievement of sending a rocket to the moon in our own day.

One can only presume that the various art motifs individually and collectively placed on the stones of Newgrange, and many of the other 43 passage-tombs in the eastern part of the country, must have been applied 32 in connection with the ritual or religion of the builders, for the art on these stones is more than just doodling. It represents an intentional collection of motifs, some of which have already been mentioned in connection with other passage-tombs.

The lozenge and zigzag are frequently found on the Newgrange stones, but more than any other, Newgrange gives prominence to the spiral, present only on Irish passage-tombs, and which is found in its unique triple form not only on the hindmost niche, but also on the great stone in 45 front of the entrance, a composition which must surely be hailed as one of 42 the finest pieces of stonecarving in the whole of prehistoric Europe. What

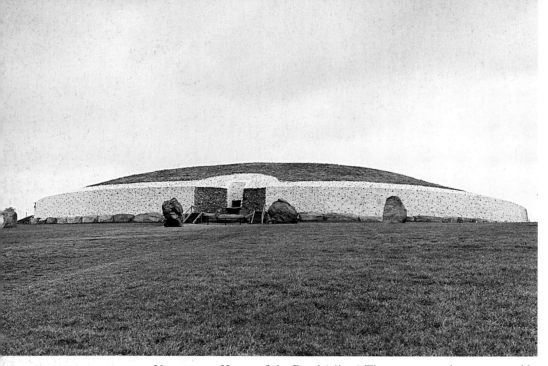

**44–47 Newgrange, House of the Dead** (*Above*) The reconstructed monument with its white quartz façade. (*Below*) Inside the tomb chamber, looking down the passage towards the entrance. (*Opposite, above*) The beam-walled roof of the chamber. (*Opposite, below*) The highly decorated roofstone above the eastern burial recess in the chamber.

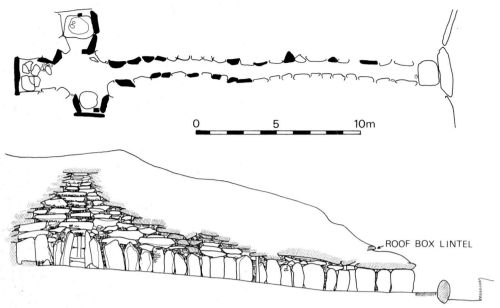

ROOF BOX LINTEL

48,49 **Newgrange in perspective** (*Above*) Plan and section of the tomb. (*Below*) Overall plan of the mound.

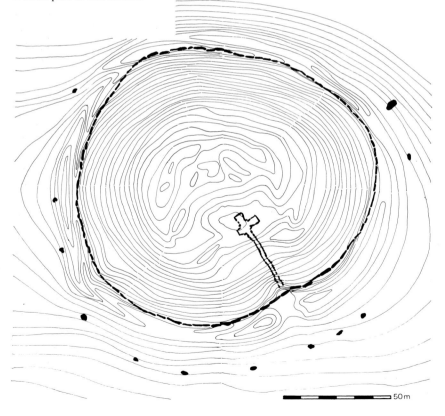

50 m

50 Stylized human face on a stone in the passage-tomb at Fourknocks, Co. Meath.

these various symbols mean is a matter of frequent speculation. One can argue, for instance, that the spiral follows the sun's movement, and the serpentiform the moon's, but we have no Rosetta stone to give us the key to their meaning. Down the centuries stone is usually the last – but also the most enduring – material on which designs have been applied, and it may not be too fanciful to surmise that many of the motifs of passage-tomb art may have been used earlier on other material – wood, or even tapestries or weavings of the kind found in folk art throughout the world but which, in the case of the passage-tomb builders, may have been used in decorating the interiors of the houses of the living.

While almost the whole treasury of motifs is purely geometric in design, there are some stones in passage-tomb art which must surely be seen as anthropomorphic. One of these is in the tomb at Fourknocks, Co. Meath, some 9 miles southeast of Newgrange. There, in a passage-tomb with a short passage but a remarkably large burial chamber, Patrick Hartnett discovered a stone incised with what can only be described as a stylized human face, crossed below by a half-moon shape which could be taken as a mouth, but which might conceivably represent a neck ornament of some kind. Was this intended as a memorial to one of the dead buried in the tomb, or could it even represent a god? If the passage-tomb builders worshipped any single god, surely that god must have been the sun, whose rays shine annually into the Newgrange tomb. It must be more than idle speculation to suggest that the rayed circle, found particularly at Loughcrew, might represent the sun, and the round shape of the passage-tomb might also reflect the orb of the sun. 50 32

If Newgrange and Knowth were built at roughly the same time – and Dowth is unlikely to differ very much in date – how are we to explain that three such giant mounds came to be built so close in time and space to one another? Are we to envisage a society whose pharaoh-like leader kept the minds of his people from rebellious or warlike thoughts by getting them to build pyramids in the round? Do the tombs represent the products of three separate socially élite and hierarchical groups in the surrounding territory, each vying with the other in pomp and circumstance? Or should we see these three great mounds as triple cathedrals forming the centrepieces in an area sanctified by ritual along the lower reaches of the Boyne which, as we shall see in the next chapter, also continued to play some very special role in the second millennium bc as well?

The Boyne Valley is unique in its passage-tomb richness, but other significant megalithic groupings including passage-tombs also occur, for instance, in Brittany and in the Orkneys. Comparisons for the Irish art motifs are found on Orkney pottery, and on a single exotic passage-tomb in Brittany, namely Gavrinis. These art connections have led to the suggestion that the people who built the great Boyne Valley tombs may have come up the Irish Sea in considerable numbers from Brittany, and ultimately from the Iberian Peninsula, where good parallels are known for tombs such as Fourknocks, and where there are also occasional instances of similarities in the gravegoods.

The Irish passage-tombs have structural characteristics which relate them to a broad family of similar graves strung out along the Atlantic coast of Europe, of which the earliest known appear to have been built in Brittany around 3800 bc. But the gravegoods of the Irish passage-tombs seem to be distinctively native, and the art of the Boyne Valley tombs which has prompted the suggestion of their having connections with Brittany and the Iberian Peninsula occurs on monuments which represent the zenith of development rather than the beginnings of Irish passage-tomb architecture.

What, then, of the origin of the earliest Irish passage-tombs? The undifferentiated tomb, Site 16, at Knowth, which was earlier than the main mound, bears little art upon its stones, while the example at Townleyhall close by, with a radiocarbon date of c.2730, has no art at all. Equally lacking in art is Grave 27 at Carrowmore, a passage-less cruciform chamber with gravegoods akin to those of the passage-tombs, and to which its Swedish excavators assigned an even earlier date in the late fourth millennium bc, on the basis of radiocarbon samples. It depends upon our interpretation of the Carrowmore findings whether we see the passage-less cruciform chamber of Grave 27 as being a late fourth millennium precursor of the Irish passage-tomb, or whether we see the undifferentiated tomb as the earliest form developing early in the third millennium, and leading on to the type with cruciform ground-plan as constructed at Newgrange around the middle of the third millennium bc.

82

While the idea of building passage-tombs may ultimately be of Breton origin, we do not have to envisage an entire 'flotilla' coming from Brittany, peopling Ireland with a new race which built a whole range of passage-tombs there. A sedentary Neolithic population had been present in Ireland for half a millennium before megaliths were constructed there, and while it may have needed some impetus from outside to establish the idea, we must envisage the possibility that it was an already long-established people who were responsible for building most of the passage-tombs of Ireland, without necessarily seeing the Mesolithic population as having made a significant contribution to their development.

If we confine ourselves to the relative dates for the development of court cairns and passage-tombs, the radiocarbon determinations current-ly available would suggest that the court cairns are marginally earlier. The differing ground-plans found in these two major types could be seen as belonging to two different sections of the population whose geographical distribution was largely but not entirely disparate. They can be seen to coalesce neatly in Cairn E at Carrowkeel and in those court cairns in Mayo and Sligo which have transepts. Further intermingling is suggested in the chalk ball with passage-tomb affinities found in the court cairn at Creevykeel, Co. Sligo, as well as in the decoration on the stones of the court cairn at Malin, Co. Donegal, if it was applied at the time when the tomb was built, rather than having been added in the Iron Age, as some believe. An alternative explanation for the difference between the two major types of tomb was suggested by Estyn Evans, who saw them (perhaps influenced by modern Ireland) as representing different religious beliefs, the court cairns belonging, as he saw it, to a 'northern region, eschewing iconography', and the passage-tombs to a 'more artistic, flamboyant, sun-worshipping south'. 23, 36, 49 28

But the very fact that the northern half of the country is rich in court cairns and passage-tombs, while the southern half has very few Neolithic megaliths in comparison, leads inevitably to the question as to why megaliths were built in certain areas and not in others? The same problem applies on the European Continent, where megaliths can be seen as being a predominantly Western and Northern European phenomenon, whereas Southeastern and Central Europe are practically devoid of them. Colin Renfrew, Richard Bradley and Ian Kinnes, among others, have been making efforts during the last decade to explain the rationale behind the building of megaliths, and the ideas of these English scholars might well also be applicable to Ireland. 19

The megalithic tombs are seen as symbols of social cohesion, expressions of territorial behaviour in small-scale sedentary societies; they were built as public centres and meeting places, competing with those of other segments of society not involved in the building of the tombs. They represent a focal monument to embody the communal aspirations and the right to ancestral lands surrounding the tombs. They are the repositories of the remains of the community's ancestors, and the greater the respect shown to the ancestral dead in the size of their tombs, the more important was the standing of the living community. Possessing the ancestors meant possession of the land they held for many generations, and any other resources which may be available in the locality. Pressure on this land and its resources, and the need to establish tribal identity, only arises where the population is threatened by stress of some sort, brought about by warlike tendencies in a society with increasing population numbers. Signs of just such stress may have been present in Middle Neolithic times in Atlantic Europe, where the tombs are common in areas of secondary settlement, when society was beginning to burst at the seams. Where further expansion westwards was impeded by the ocean, as in Ireland or the Orkneys, for instance, populations were under greatest stress; the more marginal the area, the more important became the claims for land, hence the larger the tombs.

The intervention of ancestors in the spiritual world could also have been seen as helping to contribute to the agricultural surplus throughout the whole area of the community served by the tomb, though only a few were presumably considered important enough to find a lasting resting place in a megalithic tomb. It may be, too, that the fact that there is evidence in a number of cases for bodies having been buried elsewhere for a time before their bones were finally laid to rest might be explained by the hypothesis that it was only after defleshing that the body could pass into the spiritual world.

Physical possession of the bones of the ancestral dead could thus have been used as a tool to gain power over available resources. By cremating the bones (the type of burial most common in Irish megaliths), the ancestral bones could be prevented from falling into the wrong hands. Another mechanism possibly used to gain control over existing resources was the possession of, and perhaps even the magic attached to, exclusive objects which can, if necessary, be destroyed by being taken out of circulation – in times of potential danger, for instance. The deposition of 37, 38 the exotic flint macehead at Knowth may be explained by such an hypothesis, though rare and beautiful objects could also have been exchanged as gifts among communities in order to gain their alliance against a common foe, or to establish the donor as the most important individual in certain sectors of a wealthy society. As pressure on critical resources increased, and contact with the European mainland diminished in time, independent traditions of formal burial within a fragmented society may have led to the development of different varieties of tomb, while at the same time retaining a broad range of similar gravegoods deposited with the dead.

Such theories, sometimes evolved from modern ethnographic parallels, represent a step forward in trying to explain the phenomenon of megalithic tombs. But the large areas of Ireland devoid of megalithic

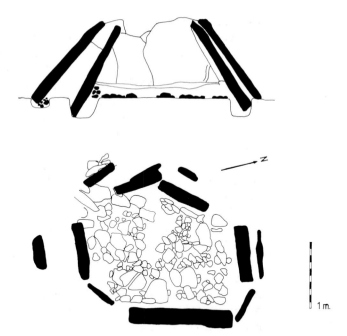

51 Section and plan of the Neolithic grave at Jerpoint West, Co. Kilkenny.

tombs during the Neolithic period show that the theories would apply only to those areas where megalithic tombs are present. The virtual absence of such tombs in the southern half of the country does not imply that the area was uninhabited: rather, we should presume that the pressures which caused megaliths to be built in the northern half of the country were largely absent in the southern half, where burials of a simpler nature occur.

## The first single-grave burials

The unremarkable Neolithic burials found in pits at places such as Martinstown, Co. Meath and at Site C at Lough Gur in Co. Limerick, may well be of the kind widely practised in the southern half of Ireland during the Neolithic period, where a lack of datable gravegoods would make many single burials unrecognizable as Neolithic in date. But, in addition, a very distinctive group of Neolithic single burials has recently crystallized which are very different from the megalithic tombs, though the two groups have certain constructional and other links. These have become known as burials of 'Linkardstown' type, after the classic example in Co. Carlow, which was excavated by Joseph Raftery around 1944. The burials are usually of a single adult male, occasionally accompanied by another burial (once of a child), and with the bones sometimes in a disarticulated condition, suggesting that they had been given a temporary resting place elsewhere before final deposition. In the case of Jerpoint 51 West, Co. Kilkenny, excavated by Michael Ryan, cremated remains were also found, and animal bones occur occasionally too. The burials were placed in a massive stone cist, generally polygonal in shape and having a paved floor, with the walls of the cist made of stones – often doubled or trebled – which all sloped inwards towards the centre. The cists were covered with single, or two overlapping, stones. They were usually placed centrally in a round mound consisting of earth, stones and also often of carefully laid sods, and occasionally the mound had a small kerb of low stones. The cairn at Poulawack, Co. Clare, ought probably to be included in this group, although its central cist held the remains of four individuals, and its mound contained a number of other apparently primary cists. In addition to undecorated 'Western Neolithic' pottery, these graves usually produced one round-bottomed pot which frequently had a large-necked rim. These pots were distinguished by their ample decoration, often arranged in zones, as in the example from Jerpoint West, or in a series of overlapping concentric grooved arcs as found on the pot which Barry Raftery excavated at Baunogenasraid, Co. Carlow, though other decorative motifs also occur. In addition, small bone pins with a rounded knob at the top were found, as well as a flint arrowhead or a polished stone axe and, in one instance, a bead.

'Linkardstown' burials are concentrated in an area stretching from Dublin to counties Carlow and Kilkenny, but allied monuments are scattered in counties Tipperary, Limerick and Clare. This small group of burials, amounting thus far to less than a dozen satisfactorily identified examples, was for long dated to the end of the Neolithic period (say, around 2000 bc), resulting in the notion that they were the scarce precursors of the single burials of the Early Bronze Age. But recent radiocarbon dates for some of these sites have shown that they can now be placed firmly in the middle of the Neolithic. The dates are as follows: Ardcrony, Co. Tipperary – c.2725 bc; Ballintruer More, Co. Wicklow – c.2850 bc; Ashley Park, Co. Tipperary (a slightly atypical example) – c.2815 bc; and an as yet unpublished date for Poulawack turns out to be only a little younger. These dates are closely comparable to those for passage-tombs – though earlier than Knowth or Newgrange – to which their round mounds and central burials, as well as their gravegoods, would seem to relate them, and they show that single-grave burial in polygonal cists was being practised at the same time as the collective burial in passage-tombs. They are not, however, necessarily ancestral to the cist burials of the Earlier Bronze Age, which are discussed in the next chapter.

# 4·The Rise of Metalworking

THE GREAT MIDDLE NEOLITHIC passage-tombs of the Boyne Valley were too gigantic and too prominent in the landscape to fall into oblivion for too long. The fascination which they have been exercising over our imagination in recent years is just the latest example of the magic spell which these mounds have been casting since they were built, for they have continued to attract both pagan and Christian down the centuries. Indeed, the pagan mythology associated with them, which survived in oral tradition long enough to be written down in the Middle Ages, gives us some hint of the central cult role which they must have played for succeeding generations, some of whom actually lived in the shadow of these great monuments. Knowth was fortified in the early years AD, and became the royal seat of the kings of northern Brega in the ninth century AD. At Newgrange, numerous finds of Roman coins and gold jewellery of the first few Christian centuries were surely more than just 'coins in a fountain', and must have been the votive offerings of people who came from within the bounds of the Roman Empire to do homage to the god(s) of Newgrange. 33

After Newgrange's floruit in the middle centuries of the third millennium bc, the spirit of its builders would appear to have waned – a victim of the ineluctable decline and fall of even the strongest civilizations. Even if Newgrange may have continued to serve its original function for a considerable time, not many centuries after its completion the outer layers of the mound slipped down over the great kerbstones which had been designed to keep them in place. (It was, incidentally, to put the clock back on this slipping that the recent restoration of the façade of Newgrange was undertaken, in an effort to give some idea of how Newgrange must have impressed people when it was first built about 5,000 years ago.) After these initial signs of decay, however, a small settlement grew up around the periphery of the mound. Its inhabitants built some rectangular structures with walls of wood or wattle, and roofs of thatch, one of which showed traces of a fierce fire. A number of hearths suggest that, in addition, there may also have been some rather more flimsy constructions as well, but these have long since disappeared. Charcoal discovered in these secondary settlement remains at Newgrange provided material for a number of radiocarbon dates for the domestic activity there, and these ranged over a period of almost two centuries from c.2100 to c.1925 bc, the beginning of the Earlier Bronze Age. 44

The Newgrange settlement also yielded a considerable quantity of animal bones which have been examined by Louise van Wijngaarden-Bakker of Amsterdam, and her study has given us our most detailed review of the animal bones associated with any prehistoric site in Ireland. The vast majority of bones belonged to domestic animals. Sheep and goat played only a minimal role, and most of the bones were those of cattle and pigs, the latter of which were, like the dog, present in Ireland since the Mesolithic. But a newcomer was the horse, which had only recently been introduced into Western Europe at the time, and which was perhaps used to round up and control cattle as they were moved from summer to winter feeding grounds, and back again. Wild animals, which comprised only 2 per cent of all the bones, included red deer, mountain hare and wild cat. There was evidence in Michael J. O'Kelly's excavation that the meat of some of these animals had been stored in some of the many pits which were found around the periphery of the great mound.

Yet the thousands of animal bones found in the Newgrange settlement ought not to be interpreted as indicating that those who lived there after the mound had begun to slip concentrated solely on pasturage. For one of the pits also contained charred grains of naked barley and emmer wheat, which doubtless represented two of the most important crops in prehistoric Ireland. The reappearance of grass and plantain in the pollen spectrum of the later third millennium bc suggests renewed activity in land-clearance, but there is also some evidence that the climate was becoming damper, and that Neolithic farmers in upland areas may have been forced by encroaching bog to seek alternative land at lower levels.

Michael J. O'Kelly's excavation of this settlement at Newgrange also produced a number of interesting items, such as a bronze axe and the segment of a large double arc of pits, which we will have reason to return to later. A considerable quantity of small finds were uncovered, too, including worked stone and myriads of potsherds. The stonework – mostly flint tools, but there were also stone axes – showed signs of continuity with that used by the tomb-builders centuries earlier. But cf. 18 apart from some sherds of Carrowkeel ware characteristic of the passage-tombs, most of the pottery found was of a kind which represents a break with the older tradition. The few pots which can be reasonably well reconstructed show them to have been flat-bottomed vessels with sides rising in a gentle curve, sometimes S-shaped, and with a wide variety of decoration. This consists often of bands of horizontal lines of grooves or cord-impressions, occasionally with the addition of zones of hatching, cross-hatching or herring-bone. Along with this decorated ware, there was also much coarser pottery which bore no ornamentation, as well as 52 one exotic shape – the polypod bowl, a thick-walled vessel to which four feet were added separately. Most of the sherds from the Newgrange settlement belong to what is described as Beaker pottery, for scholars in the past believed it was used for quaffing alcoholic beverages.

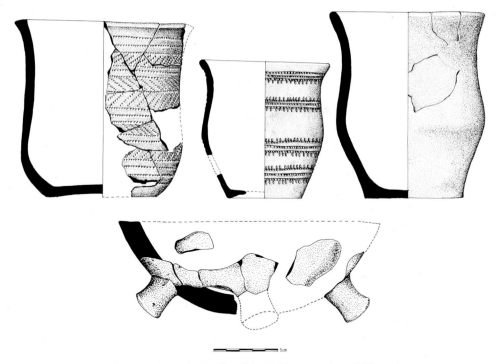

52 Beaker pottery from, left to right, Dalkey Island; Newgrange; and Knowth; together with fragments of a polypod bowl from Newgrange.

## Beaker pots and Beaker makers

Half a century ago, scarcely any of this Beaker pottery was known from Ireland at all. But since then, excavations at Lough Gur and at many sites in the northern half of Ireland, have helped to fill out the picture of its original distribution. Occasionally, it has been found in wedge-tombs (a type of megalith to be discussed below), but most of this Beaker pottery has come from settlement sites, of which Newgrange is only one. Not surprisingly, the next-door tumulus at Knowth is another. Here, Beaker pottery was uncovered in four separate concentrations together with pits and post-holes, but there were no definite traces of houses or any permanent structures. One of these concentrations proved to consist largely of coarsish pottery, but the other three had finer ware bearing decoration resembling, but not as varied as, that at Newgrange. In the passage of one of the satellite tombs (Site 15), Knowth produced the only example hitherto known in Ireland of a burial definitely associated with Beaker pottery. This was an undecorated Bell Beaker with the cremated remains of an adult and a child. Newgrange and Knowth were not the only earlier settlement sites which were later occupied by the makers of Beaker pottery. The Late Mesolithic site on Dalkey Island in Dublin Bay had a shell midden associated with Beaker ware. Ballynagilly, Co. Tyrone, first occupied in the Neolithic, saw three separate settlement sites on the flanks of the hill-top, where hearths, pits and post- and stake-holes were found,

52

36

52
9

89

but nothing which could be called a house. The radiocarbon dates for these settlements range between $c.2010$ and 1900 bc – thus tallying well with those for Newgrange. Oval houses at Site D at Lough Gur have been claimed to belong to the period of use of the Beaker pottery there.

cf. 14

Houses which can be associated with the makers of Beaker pottery are, indeed, very rare in Europe, despite the extensive use of this pottery type over vast areas of the Continent – from Hungary to Portugal, and from Denmark to Sicily – where it is frequently found in conjunction with single inhumation burials, early metalwork, and also with the introduction of the horse. The origins of this pottery have been claimed variously for regions as far apart as the Iberian Peninsula, Central Europe and the Low Countries, and it has been suggested that a short-headed skull type often buried with Beakers may be interpreted as heralding the spread of a new race of people. But Colin Burgess, Stephen Shennan and others have recently cast considerable doubt on this old assumption, and have suggested instead that Beakers for beer-drinking, and many of the artefacts that were eventually associated with them, represented not the accoutrements of people who expanded rapidly over large areas of Europe, but rather a prestige 'cult package' or fashion spread by culture contact or commerce.

The earliest Beakers in England – those with all-over cord-decoration in horizontal lines – seem to have derived directly from the Low Countries around 2150 bc, and these are fairly generally recognized as having been introduced by newly arrived people, though in what numbers it is obviously difficult to judge. These first British Beakers were followed a century and a half later by others with comb-decoration, also in horizontal bands. Subsequently, local styles developed in Britain, with the original S-curved wall-shapes giving way to more angular varieties, first with short and later with long-necked vessels which often betray vertically panelled elements in their decoration. Many of the reconstructible Beaker pots from Ireland fit best into the somewhat more developed types of Beakers in Britain, though the polypod bowls from Newgrange are exotics which suggest more direct contacts with the Continent.

52

In certain aspects, the features of Irish Beakers do not, for some as yet unexplained reason, follow the usual pattern of development in Britain. Beaker pottery is, for example, little known from settlement sites in Central Europe and Britain, whereas in Ireland, most of the Beaker pottery is found associated with domestic activity, as we have seen at Newgrange, Knowth, Ballynagilly, Dalkey Island and Lough Gur. A further difference is that the single inhumation Beaker burial, as known widely in Britain, has not yet been recognized in Ireland, where the unique double cremation with an undecorated Beaker in the Site 15 passage-tomb at Knowth is its closest counterpart. However, the long-established practice of cremation in Ireland may well have been responsible for stemming any enthusiasm for the Beaker variety of single

36

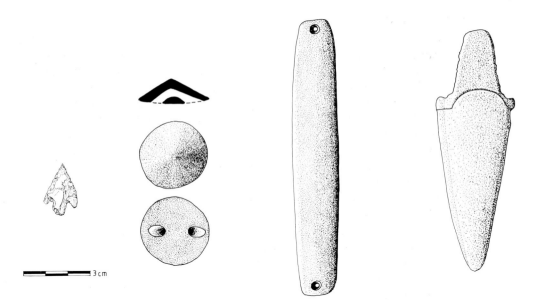

53 'Beaker-compatible' objects: from left, barbed and tanged flint arrowhead, Rathlin Island, Co. Antrim; jet V-perforated button, Lissan, Co. Tyrone/Fermanagh; stone archer's wrist guard or bracer, Lough Gur, Co. Limerick; and tanged copper dagger, Knocknagur, Co. Galway.

inhumation burial though, as we have seen, Ireland had earlier practised single inhumation around the middle of the third millennium bc. Where Beaker pottery is found in a burial context in Ireland, it is largely associated with megaliths of the wedge variety. This connection between Beakers and megaliths is, however, also something which Ireland shares in common with Brittany and other areas of Atlantic Europe, where Bell Beakers, popular in Ireland, are also found.

The features associated with the presence of Beaker pottery may thus combine elements from two distinct geographical areas – Britain and Atlantic Europe. But while the finding of Beaker pottery associated with habitation sites rather than with individual burials is a trait connecting Ireland with Atlantic shores further south, the concentration of Beaker material in the northern half of Ireland would argue for a stronger connection with Britain and, ultimately, therefore, with Central rather than Western Europe. This predilection for the northern half of Ireland in the distribution of Beaker pottery can also be followed in items such as the tanged copper dagger, archers' wrist guards and the V-perforated buttons, which are usually associated with Beaker pottery in Britain and on the Continent, though never found together with it in Ireland. The distribution of another typical Beaker object, the barbed-and-tanged flint arrowhead, is likely to follow the same pattern. Why these objects are not found with Beaker pottery in Ireland may be because the latter may have been past its prime before these 'Beaker compatible' objects came into common use in Ireland, or because the Irish were not yet ready to renew the increasingly popular custom of burial in single graves where these

53

objects and the Beaker pottery could have been deposited together. But it is perhaps premature to be sure whether the advent of Beaker pottery brought with it incursions of new 'Beaker people' (if such existed), or whether the novel pottery type was merely adopted by an already long-established local population which considered it to be a necessary adjunct to the drinking of some newly introduced alcoholic beverage such as ale or mead. The explanation of native adaptation could find support in the strong local tradition evident in the stonework and the grits used in the pottery of the Beaker settlement at Newgrange.

### Henge-like monuments

One rather unusual type of monument in the Boyne Valley where Beaker
33  pottery was used was the round earthen enclosure at Monknewtown, Co. Meath, excavated by David Sweetman. A flat central area here was surrounded originally by a now largely ploughed-out round earthen bank about 1.5 m high, which must have measured about 96 m in diameter. Inside the northern part of the bank, Sweetman uncovered twelve burials, mainly in pits, some of which had upright stone settings, and one was covered by a large capstone. Some of the pits contained cremated bone, but others which did not may once have held inhumed burials long disappeared in the soil. Only small quantities of pottery were found in the burials, but one pot discovered was found to be flat-bottomed while
cf. 18  another was a round-bottomed Carrowkeel bowl, typical of passage-tombs. In the southern part of the enclosure, a large oval hollow in the ground was found to contain an irregular series of post-hole settings, together with a hearth. From this it was possible to reconstruct a pit-house with supporting posts which probably held up a thatched roof. Around this house a variety of potsherds was found, some of which bore
cf. 52  ornament comparable to that on Beakers. Others were plain, and suggested ascription to the so-called 'rusticated Beaker' which may, however, only have a remote connection with actual decorated Beaker pottery. Charcoal from the hearth gave a radiocarbon date of c.1860 bc, which is only marginally later than that for the Beaker pottery in the settlement around the base of the Newgrange mound. The discovery of the Carrowkeel bowl among the graves raises the question as to whether the graves may have been earlier than the settlement with Beaker pottery, or whether Monknewtown was a roughly contemporary unit with people associated with the passage-tomb builders burying their dead in pits, and using pottery of Beaker type as well as domesticated ware which may have had little to do with Beaker.

Monknewtown is the sole excavated example of a number of such round-banked enclosures found in the Boyne Valley. These may have served as a cult centre and focal meeting point for the population of the surrounding territory, but the fact that Monknewtown is just one of a number of similar henge-like monuments in the same general area only helps to emphasize that the Boyne Valley was one of the – if not indeed *the* – most important cult centre of the later Stone Age and the emerging Bronze Age in Ireland.

That the Valley has many more secrets to yield in support of this contention is demonstrated by a similar, but even more curious monument – this time right beside Newgrange itself. During his excavations to the southeast of the great mound there, Michael J. O'Kelly uncovered a series of large pits (now marked by cement posts) which formed a small segment of a whole circle having a diameter of about 90 m, thus marginally smaller than Monknewtown. This circle enclosed one of Newgrange's satellite passage-tombs known as Site Z. Subsequently, David Sweetman uncovered further segments of this great arc, the outermost pits of which contained large wooden stakes. Inside these were pits of varying sizes, some of which contained cremated animal remains – though never enough to have made up a whole animal. Some of these pits were marked by standing stones which had subsequently been removed.

Within the great circle were traces of domestic activity, and radiocarbon dates for these and the post-holes corresponded well with those obtained by O'Kelly for the Beaker habitation immediately beside it, suggesting to Sweetman that the circle was built at the same time as the domestic Beaker activity on the site. The reconstruction of this monument indicates a large double circle of wooden posts, in which portions of animals were cremated and buried in rows of pits. Despite the presence of domestic refuse within, this double circle of posts with its animal cremation pits smacks of being a sacrificial cult centre, almost as important in its day as the great mound beside it had been half a millennium before. The nature of its ritual eludes us, but it may have been related to that practised in the contemporary henges of southern England which, like the Newgrange circle overlooking the Boyne, was presumably the expression of common public enterprise – analogous to the modern church – in erecting a focal meeting place independent of the tribal burial place.

In the adjoining field to the east at Newgrange, there is a large U-shaped monument which could be related to the wooden circle, but it may be more closely connected to the great passage-tomb, because a similar monument on the Hill of Tara, the so-called 'Banqueting Hall' – a long sunken area resembling a Greek stadium in shape – seems to be a ritual roadway leading directly to the passage-tomb there known as the Mound of the Hostages.

136

One further interesting point to emerge from Sweetman's recent excavations was that one of the large, roughly hewn stones of the partial circle of stones surrounding a part of the great passage-tomb at Newgrange was probably erected later than the wooden circle, so that we can now dismiss the partial circle of standing stones as having anything to do with the great mound which they enclose.

44

## Stone circles

Whatever religious ceremonies may have been enacted at Newgrange or Monknewtown, they were not confined either to the Boyne Valley or to the Beaker-using period, as the presence of other circular structures found in other parts of Ireland demonstrates. One of these is the great circle in Grange townland, Co. Limerick, excavated by Seán P. Ó Ríordáin as part of a large-scale programme in the Lough Gur area, which brought to light the Stone Age houses on Knockadoon, not half a mile away. Here, there was an impressive circle of stones reaching a height of up to 3 m, outside which was a 9/10-m-wide earthen bank with large portal stones at the inner end of its eastern entrance. The area within the circle was raised about 50 cm above the old ground level by a special flooring of clay. The pottery found both in the bank and in the circular area which it enclosed proved to have been much the same as that from the Lough Gur houses on Knockadoon – Lough Gur Class I and II ware largely of Neolithic date, as well as Beaker and Food Vessel (see below) – a collection of Stone and Bronze Age wares which suggested to the excavator that the circle was erected in the Beaker-using period.

The combination of earthen bank and stone circle at Grange, which might help to define this monument as a 'henge', links it nevertheless to more than 200 stone circles found grouped in specific parts of Ireland. Of these, almost 100 are concentrated in the southwestern counties of Cork and Kerry. Here, the circles are very much smaller, many of them consisting of no more than five stones, though the number can, on occasion, rise to nineteen. One peculiarity shared by a number of them is the presence of an axial stone lying horizontally in the southwestern quadrant of the circle, opposite the entrance where the tallest of the stones are located. A large monolith sometimes stands inside or outside the circle, and occasionally an alignment of standing stones is found in association with the monument. Four of the six circles excavated in the southwest have produced evidence of a cremation burial within the circle, that at Drombeg in Co. Cork being contained in a flat-bottomed pot which had been intentionally broken before its deposition. But whether these burials were associated with the original use of the circle, or were a subsequent addition, must remain an open question. A leaf-shaped and a barbed-and-tanged arrowhead from the circle at Cashelkeelty in Co. Kerry helped to link it with the Beaker-using period, but radiocarbon dates which its excavator, Ann Lynch, obtained at other sites suggested at least the continued use – whatever about the building – of these stone circles as late as the first millennium bc. Slightly unexpected in the southwest of Ireland is the presence of four-stone 'circles' known as 'Four Posters', which find their closest counterparts in northern England and in Scotland.

The stone circles of Cork and Kerry have been analyzed to see if there is any possibility of their having played a part in recording the movement of

54

54 Drombeg stone circle, Co. Cork.

celestial bodies, such as the sun or moon. The extension of a line drawn between the middle of the entrance and the centre of the axial stone opposite was checked to verify whether it corresponded to a point on either horizon at which the sun or moon or some obvious star rose or fell on some significant day of the year, such as midwinter or midsummer day, or on one of the equinoxes half-way between them. John Barber maintained that there was a high degree of probability that the main axes of a significant number of stone circles were orientated on important solar and lunar events – Drombeg, for instance, being orientated on the midwinter sunset. But P.R. Freeman and W. Elmore claimed that Barber's data did not support any hypothesis of purposeful astronomical orientation. Although Ann Lynch believes that the stone alignments may well have significant lunar orientations, the possibility of stone circles having acted as prehistoric 'observatories' must await further proof. Yet surely only two stones, and not a whole stone circle with entrance and axial stone, is all that would have been necessary to mark a point of astronomical significance upon the horizon, and some other purpose must have been intended originally for the use of the circular form – possibly in connection with the worship of the rounded orb of the sun? 54

55 Stone circle known as 'The Piper's Stones' at Athgreany, Co. Wicklow.

Near the northwestern end of the Wicklow Hills, in the eastern part of Ireland, there is another group of stone circles. One of these, at Castleruddery in Co. Wicklow, resembles the circle in Grange townland near Lough Gur in having a stone-lined bank, an eastern entrance and **55** portal stones. The circle at Athgreany, also in Co. Wicklow, with a large stone standing outside the circle, is one of two in this group called 'The Piper's Stones', a name which enshrines the old legend of the piper (the standing stone) and his dancers pirouetting in a circle who were turned into stone for having dared to amuse themselves so frivolously on the Sabbath – an obvious survival of more puritanical days 300 years ago.

One of a group of apparent henges on the open heath known as the Curragh in Co. Kildare, had a central oval pit containing the skeleton of a young woman who showed signs of having been buried alive! Features of the skeleton were unusual: the head was probably upright; one hand and one leg were pressed against the side of the grave; and the legs were apart. In the same general area, there are also some standing stones, including **56** one over 7 m tall at Punchestown in Co. Kildare, which is the second highest anywhere in Britain or Ireland. It had a stone cist at its foot which proved to be empty, but a cist at the foot of a standing stone associated with a 'henge' monument known as the Longstone Rath, at Furness in Co. **cf. 53** Kildare, contained a stone two-holed archer's wrist guard, suggesting that the stone may have been erected during or not much later than the period when Beaker pottery was in use in Ireland. The purpose of standing stones is as enigmatic as that of stone circles; some suggest that they may have marked burials, others explain them as markers along prehistoric trackways, while Estyn Evans, wryly but correctly, remarked that some were erected as late as the last century to enable cattle to scratch themselves!

56 The 7-m-high standing stone at Punchestown, Co. Kildare, is the tallest in Ireland. ▷

Outside Cork and Kerry, the other great concentration of stone circles in Ireland is found in central and southwestern Ulster in the north of Ireland, where they are only marginally larger than those in the southwest. But, in contrast, they consist of up to forty-five stones. They are frequently found near megaliths, and sometimes they occur in groups, occasionally having a stone alignment attached to them at a tangent. The most remarkable cluster of all is in the Sperrin Mountains, at Beaghmore near Cookstown in Co. Tyrone. Here, three pairs of circles and a further single example have been brought to light from beneath their covering of peat-bog, and more may yet remain to be uncovered there. At the eastern end of the site, four rows of standing stones converge on a mound which contained a Tievebulliagh axe, the mound being placed between two large, though irregular, circles. Both of the other paired circles are associated with burial cairns, one of which may be earlier than the circles. The large single circle, more oval than circular in shape, has its centre studded with 884 small stones, and it incorporates a stone cairn which interrupts the circle. There are also a number of separate cairns not directly related to the stone circles or alignments. One of these provided radiocarbon samples which gave a date between $c.1535$ and 775 bc, and as the excavator presumed the whole complex to be roughly contemporary, the building of the circles is likely to fall within this time-span. It has not proved possible to demonstrate any persuasive astronomical alignment, though Professor Thom considered that a series of four stones some distance away could have been used to observe the upper limb of the rising moon about 1640 BC.

The northern province of Ulster has a goodly share of enigmatic round monuments incorporating burials which, however, need not necessarily be contemporary. At Ballynahatty, Co. Down, the Giant's Ring consisted of a 4-m-high bank enclosing a circular area, 200 m in diameter, in the centre of which was a portal tomb with cremated bone. The ring may well be termed a 'henge', and the same may also be said of the bank with internal ditch at Dun Ruadh, in Co. Tyrone, which measured almost 60 m by 50 m in extent. Inside it, though probably a later addition, was an oval setting of stones with a burial cairn and cists associated with Bronze Age pottery. At Ballynoe, Co. Down, the Dutch excavator, Albert Egges van Giffen, found a stone circle surrounded by a long mound with a tripartite chamber at one end and a single one at the other, the mound itself being partially enclosed by a low and incomplete circular setting of stones. This setting was apparently later than a number of small round-topped stones called baetyls, of a kind also found at Knowth. Despite the finding of one pottery sherd resembling the Carrowkeel bowl from Monknewtown, the relative chronology of the various parts of this monument still baffles us, though the stone circle may well have been the final building stage, as was also the case at Newgrange.

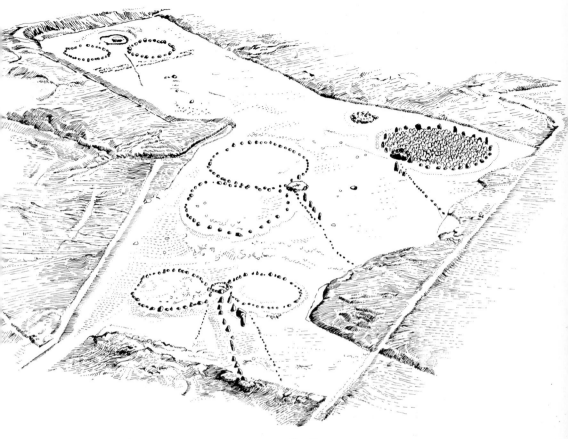

57 Bird's-eye view of the stone circles at Beaghmore, Co. Tyrone.

58 A stone circle enclosing a long mound at Ballynoe, Co. Down.

## Wedge-tombs

Another important monument type to be associated with the use of Beaker pottery is the wedge-tomb – the fourth and most numerous category of megalith in Ireland, with almost 400 examples known. It is, indeed, so widespread that Estyn Evans described it as 'the first all-Irish grave form'. Its distribution pattern, however, is not uniform, as the great majority of wedge-tombs are located to the west of a north–south line from Derry to Cork. The general northeast–southwest orientation of the wedge-tombs corresponds to that of many of the stone circles though, in contrast to the stone circles, the entrance to the wedge-tombs generally faces the southwest.

The tomb itself consists of a long narrow gallery of large upright stones covered with capstones – where they survive. The stones at the entrance are usually taller, while the remainder decline in size towards the back. The Burren area of north Co. Clare has the simplest variety, a single-chamber above-ground roofed cist without any sure evidence of a covering mound. But elsewhere, many have a separate chamber at one end of the gallery, acting either as a portico at the entrance, as at Baurnadomeeny, Co. Tipperary, or placed at the back of the burial gallery, as seen in the large and imposing example at Labbacallee, Co. Cork. Ballyedmonduff, Co. Dublin and Loughash, Cashelbane, Co. Tyrone, show a combination of both of these features. Frequently, around the sides and end of the tomb there is a setting of stones which can be heel- or U-shaped, or more fan-like towards the front: these settings may well have served to keep the covering mound in place. A rare feature is the presence of cupmarks on some of these stones. With few exceptions, the bones of the dead – sometimes demonstrably of more than one individual – were cremated.

cf. 52    One third of the nineteen excavated examples yielded Beaker pottery, that from the tomb at Moytirra in Co. Sligo being amongst the finest specimens of Bell Beaker pottery known from Ireland. But the pottery found also included flat-bottomed coarse ware, as well as Food Vessel pottery, all of which were taken in certain instances to have been contemporary; cord-ornamented ware of Case's Sandhills type was found at Boviel in Co. Derry.

cf. 53    Barbed-and-tanged arrowheads, a typically Beaker product, were found in four of the northern tombs, though flintwork of other kinds was also frequently present. The finds from the examples excavated in the north of Ireland were richer than those further south, and amongst the more exotic artefacts was what has been seen as fragments of a bone dagger pommel, and what could conceivably have formed part of a racquet-headed pin, found at Largantea in Co. Derry. Curiously, in three separate instances, parts of moulds for Bronze Age spearheads and palstaves were found. The spearhead mould from Moylisha in Co. Wicklow, of a kind which belongs to the fully fledged Bronze Age, was

19

59 Conjectural reconstruction of the wedge-tomb at Island, Co. Cork.

found at the base of the cairn. This fact, and the radiocarbon date of *c.*1160 bc for the tomb excavated at Island, Co. Cork, suggests that wedge-tombs remained in use at least until, and may even have continued to be built as late as, the last few centuries of the second millennium bc. When they were first built is a difficult question to answer, particularly as those which have been excavated have not been prolific in datable finds. That they were in existence during the Beaker pottery period is clearly demonstrated. But the presence of the cord-ornamented Sandhills ware at Boviel, and the Neolithic 'look' of some of the earliest pottery at Baurnadomeeny and in the wedge-tomb at Lough Gur, should make us aware of the possibility that some wedge-tombs may have been built before the Beaker-using period, and thus closer in time to the other megalith types discussed in the previous chapter.

De Valera postulated that the builders of wedge-tombs were a people separate from those who built court cairns, passage-tombs and portal-tombs. Seeing a comparison between the Irish wedge-tombs and the *allées couvertes* of northwestern France, he suggested that the wedge-tomb builders came from Brittany, making an Irish landing in the west Cork and Kerry areas. The lack of any sound evidence for such an introduction has led other commentators, however, to believe that wedge-tombs are an indigenous development within Ireland. Leaving aside the question as to whether the Beaker-users existed as a separate and intrusive population group, the equation of Beaker-makers and tomb-builders may not be tenable, as a number of excavated wedge-tombs produced no Beaker pottery, and also because more than half of the tombs of this type are found in the southern province of Munster where – with the exception of Lough Gur – Beaker pottery is conspicuous by its absence on excavated sites. It may be noted, too, that the wedge-tombs excavated in the postulated landing areas of the southwest produced virtually no finds at all.

De Valera has also pointed out that both wedge-tombs and stone circles occur in the west Cork area where copper mines are located. But as the excavated wedge-tombs which are closest to the copper-bearing lodes are

59

singularly lacking in metal – or indeed any other finds – it would be premature to associate the wedge-tomb builders with the makers of early copper artefacts, as the evidence is equivocal on this point. There are no copper deposits in the Burren area of Co. Clare, where wedge-tombs are numerous. De Valera was probably right in explaining the concentration of wedge-tombs there as the result of pastoralist activities, particularly winter grazing, which may have been better in prehistoric times than it is today, before deforestation caused denudation of valuable topsoil. In contrast, however, the wedge-tomb at Baurnadomeeny is only one of a number of such tombs in the Rearcross-Silvermines area of north Tipperary, where John Jackson believes that there is good reason for thinking that Early Bronze Age mining may have taken place, because of the natural presence in the ore there of arsenic, antimony and silver, a combination found in metalwork of Early Bronze Age date. There is thus nothing inherently improbable in there having been a certain overlap in time between the period of use of the wedge-tombs and what we know of

cf. 66  the mining of copper ore in west Cork (see below).

### Single graves

136  When not in wedge-tombs, or as secondary insertions in passage-tombs, as is the case with the Mound of the Hostages at Tara, the burials known from the second millennium bc are single graves. We saw in the previous chapter how single burials of Linkardstown type were already known from the middle of the third millennium bc, but there is no evidence that this small group had any direct ancestral role to play in the rise in popularity of single-grave burial during the second millennium.

60  The change from the communal burial in megalithic tombs practised in the Neolithic to the single-grave burial of the Early Bronze Age may have been brought about by the fundamental restructuring of society. The megaliths were the end-product of a building programme carried out together by members of a society which, at least as far as the passage-tombs are concerned, gives the impression of probably having been hierarchical, with burial in the tombs being reserved presumably for the upper echelons of society. It is only the henges and stone circles, which are not primarily burial monuments, which provide possible testimony to communal building activity during the Bronze Age. In contrast, the burials are individually dug into the ground, and though they sometimes occur in cemeteries, they suggest a breakdown in the social structures of the Neolithic period, and the rise in Ireland of a much more egalitarian society. The richness of contemporary graves in Wessex is not evident in Ireland, where metal gravegoods are a rarity, and where the dead were seldom accompanied by more than two pottery vessels. However, we know all too little about religious practices in Early Bronze Age Ireland to be able to say whether alterations in religious attitudes had an effect on burial practices too; in changing over to single burial, however, Ireland

was in step with similar developments taking place along much of the Atlantic coast of Europe.

The single-grave burials of the second millennium bc in Ireland take many forms. Only rarely is there any indication above ground of the presence of such a grave. Yet occasionally it is possible to see a small, low, circular mound surrounded by a ditch, as at Rathjordan, Co. Limerick, where Seán P. Ó Ríordáin found a plain-shouldered Neolithic bowl which may have accompanied a burial, and another in which Neolithic, Beaker and Food Vessel pottery appeared to be contemporary in the body of the mound, suggesting an Early Bronze Age date.

The difficulty in ascribing such mounds or ring-barrows to any one period is sufficiently well demonstrated by two separate sites. One of these was a multi-period mound, about 19 m in diameter and surrounded by a ditch, which was excavated by Michael J. O'Kelly at Moneen in Co. Cork. Initially the mound covered pits, remains of a skeleton and what the excavator interpreted as Neolithic pottery. Subsequently, a cairn with a box-like tomb of megalithic proportions was added, and in the cairn a number of inhumation burials was found, dated by the presence of Food Vessel and perhaps Beaker pottery. At some even later period, cremated bones were interred along with Bronze Age pottery – Food Vessels or Urns.

The second example, excavated by Joseph Raftery at Carrowjames, Co. Mayo, showed an even longer period of use. Here, there was a total of ten mounds spread over an area 180 by 110 m. They were mostly small and low, the largest being 8.7 m in diameter but only 50 cm in height. Some had ditches surrounding them. The burials were cremations in pits, one usually at the centre of the mound and others placed elsewhere in its core. Most of the burials were devoid of any surviving gravegoods, though some did have Bronze Age 'razors', one of which was accompanied by an cf. 64 urn. But other gravegoods consisted of glass beads probably of Iron Age type, which would date the burials to somewhere around the last few centuries bc.

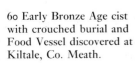
60 Early Bronze Age cist with crouched burial and Food Vessel discovered at Kiltale, Co. Meath.

Another example of a pit with cremated bone accompanied by an
64  inverted urn and a bronze 'razor' was found at Pollacurragune in Co.
Galway. Further north, a multiple-cist cairn at Mount Stewart in Co.
Down, had an empty central cist of megalithic proportions, and fifteen
cf. 61, 62  other cists in the mound, some of them containing Food Vessel pottery.
One ring-cairn at Carnkenny in Co. Tyrone provided a radiocarbon date
of *c*.865 bc.

Many of the single burials of the second millennium bc had no covering
mounds. Occasionally they showed the same proliferation of burials at
one place but – unlike the mounds at Carrowjames – these were laid out in
flat cemeteries. A good example of such a cemetery at Cloghskelt, Co.
Down, excavated by Laurence Flanagan, contained no less than twenty-
three graves. A wide variety of tomb types were shown, ranging from
burials in box-like square or rectangular cists to those without any cists at
all. One part of the cemetery had burials with Food Vessels only, while the
other parts had burials with Food Vessels and Urns of various types,
suggesting that these two types of burial pottery were used contempora-
neously. Cloghskelt is, indeed, a microcosm of the kind of flat burials
found in Ireland – particularly in the eastern half of the country – during
the second millennium bc. It was, apparently, a cremation cemetery, but
other cemeteries are known to have contained inhumed burials, while
some had both. The inhumed burials accompanied by Food Vessels were
often of people with short, rounded skulls of the kind frequently
associated elsewhere with Beaker pottery. The flat cemeteries, or indeed
flat single graves found in isolation, are widespread throughout the whole
of the island, though they are rare in the southwest. The single grave, be it
in a mound or without any indication of its presence above ground, seems
to have become popular in Ireland before the middle of the second
millennium bc, and the fashion for this kind of burial, contrasting as it
does with the megalithic communal burials, may have been introduced
from Britain. But, as John Waddell has reminded us, the question of its
origin cannot be divorced completely from that of the origin of the Food
Vessel, a pottery type often found accompanying it.

## Burial pottery: Bowls and Vases

In the foregoing paragraphs, the names Food Vessel and Urn have been
mentioned as the types of funerary pottery found in various tomb types of
the Early Bronze Age. Although the term Food Vessel may at times be a
misnomer – as the pot so-named was sometimes used not to give food to
the dead but to contain cremated ashes – the name is retained here as a
useful umbrella-term for two very different kinds of pottery – the Bowl
and the Vase – which are among the most artistic and highly decorated
wares created in prehistoric Ireland.

61  The Bowl is a semi-globular and often squat vessel, being rarely much
more than about 10 cm high. The vertical walls sometimes have two or

61 Earthen bowl-shaped
Food Vessel from Aghna-
hily, Co. Laois.

three horizontal ribs in relief, and occasionally they have a small 'waist' at
mid-height. The whole of the exterior, and sometimes even the rims and
bases, are decorated with impressed or false-relief ornament made with a
comb-like or spatulate tool. These Bowls were found accompanying – in
roughly equal proportions – both cremation and inhumation burials, in
the latter case often being placed in front of the face of the crouched corpse
deposited in stone cists. One was found at Corky, Co. Antrim, with a small
metal dagger, presumably of bronze, while polished stone axes, flints and
jet, as well as segmented faience beads were found with others. Sherds of
this decorative Bowl pottery have been found apparently with Beaker
ware, as for instance in the Rathjordan barrow mentioned above, and
Food Vessel pottery was found in a secondary position in the Mound of     136
the Hostages at Tara along with V-perforated buttons of jet which,
throughout Europe, are often associated with Beaker burials. Bowls are
also found, though in fewer numbers, in Scotland, where they may have
been inspired by the Irish potters. The typical European Beaker single-
inhumation burial is, as already stated, lacking in Ireland, and it may well
be that the Irish stone cist with inhumation burial accompanied by a Bowl
may be an Irish response to the Beaker single burial, in the same way that
the decorative Bowl, which has no obvious antecedents in Ireland, may in
some way have come into being under the stimulus of the ornamented
Beaker pottery.

Cecil P. Martin has noted that the short, rounded skulls of those buried
with Food Vessels differ from the long-skulled types known from some
Neolithic burials, thus giving rise to the suggestion that a certain influx of
people into Ireland may have been involved in the introduction of the
inhumed cist burial and the development of the Irish Bowl, a suggestion
which might help to explain the possible social and religious changes
taking place in Ireland at the same time. This is not to say, however, that

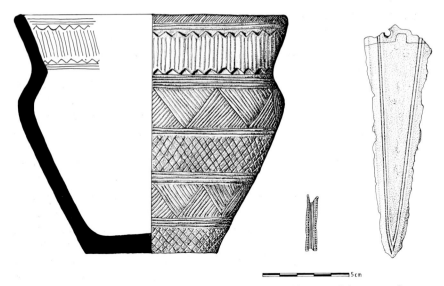

62 Vase-shaped Food Vessel and bronze dagger with gold pommel fragment, from Topped Mountain, Co. Fermanagh.

the Bowl is anything but an Irish invention. The presence of the central large cist of megalithic proportions in the multiple-cist cairn at Mount Stewart, which also had Food Vessel burials, could argue for the indigenous Neolithic population having played its part in the development of the Irish Bowl.

 Separate from, and starting probably somewhat later than the Bowl, is 62 the Vase. It is somewhat taller, though rarely higher than 16 cm, and it is richly decorated with horizontally placed incised ornament. In overall proportions, the Vase has a narrower base. The body shape can be angular or more slackly rounded, and the rim above the neck varies considerably in height. Herring-bone is frequently used as a decorative motif, though hatched triangles and simpler incised lines also occur. By the time the Vases came to be created, cremation in stone cists had become the dominant burial rite, though some Vases have also been found in simple pits. Most were apparently placed upright in the grave, though in some instances they were inverted to cover the ashes of the dead. Their association with inhumed burial is rare. It may be that the use of Vases with cremations represents the Irish reacting to the novel Bowl single inhumations by returning to the cremation rite so often practised in the megalithic tombs, but adapting it to single burial – possibly not without some contributory stimulus from England and Scotland. It is certainly noteworthy that the most important find associated with an Irish Vase was a grooved bronze dagger with gold pommel mount from Topped 62 Mountain in Co. Fermanagh, which shows affinities with daggers of the earlier portion of the Wessex culture in southern Britain. Other

associations include shells, a boar's tusk, stone beads and pendants, and also pins and needles made of bone, of which one from Corrandrum, Co. Galway, has a segmented head reminiscent of the shape of faience beads. These faience beads, of which one was found with a Vase at Ballyduff in Co. Wexford, and another with a secondary burial in the Mound of the   136
Hostages at Tara, have been the subject of much discussion as to whether they are of native insular manufacture or whether they were imported from Mediterranean lands, such as Egypt. No final agreement has been achieved on the matter.

Food Vessel burials tend, on the whole – like the Beaker pottery – to be massed in the northern half of the country, though they did spread down as far as south Leinster. They become increasingly rarer in Munster, particularly in the southwest, where many of the wedge-tombs are located. If wedge-tombs and Food Vessel cist burials were contemporary, which they may in part have been, it suggests that two very different burial rites were being practised in Ireland at the same time – perhaps by two population groups of different origins, one native and the other possibly intrusive, at least in part. The bronze dagger from Topped   62
Mountain, and another found with a Vase at Grange in Co. Roscommon, suggest that Vases were being buried with the dead around the middle of the second millennium BC. This would not be inconsistent with the radiocarbon date of *c*.1270 bc for Food Vessel sherds found in a more domestic context at Dún Ailinne in Co. Kildare.   106

## Burial pottery: Urns

The other major burial pottery type of the Earlier Bronze Age in Ireland was the Urn, which was often placed upside down over the cremated   63
remains of the dead. Some Urns were clearly associated with the Vase discussed above, and for these we may use John Waddell's term Vase Urn. Early archaeological literature often referred to them as 'Enlarged Food Vessels', for they are invariably larger than Bowl or Vase, exceeding 20 cm in height. In their overall proportions, they tend to have a much smaller base than the Bowl or Vase, and many have an angular profile with an almost vertical neck. Like the Vases, they usually bear incised ornament, consisting of herring-bone, filled triangles or lattice-motifs. The Vase Urns are found in almost equal proportions in cists and pits, though their cists tend to be more polygonal in shape, in contrast to the more rectangular type preferred in Bowl and Vase burials.

A separate type is the Encrusted Urn which, although obviously allied   63
in shape to the Vase Urns, is distinguished by the use of encrusted – or applied – zig-zag, bossed or strip ornament in relief, though frequently in conjunction with incised ornament on the upper half of the vessel. Like the Vase Urns, they are found in both pits and polygonal cists, and in a number of instances, the two Urn types were placed together in a single grave as at Corkragh (Kilskeery), Co. Tyrone. This grave also contained a

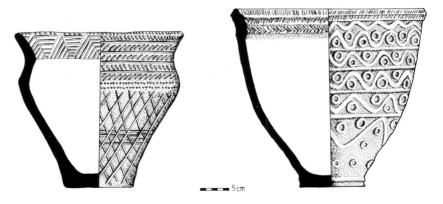

63 Vase Urn from Priest-town, Co. Down; and Encrusted Urn from Newtown, Co. Limerick.

64 Stone battle axe, bronze dagger (reconstruction) and Collared Urn from Grave XVI at Tara, Co. Meath, and bronze 'razor' with Cordoned Urn from Pollacurragune, Co. Galway.

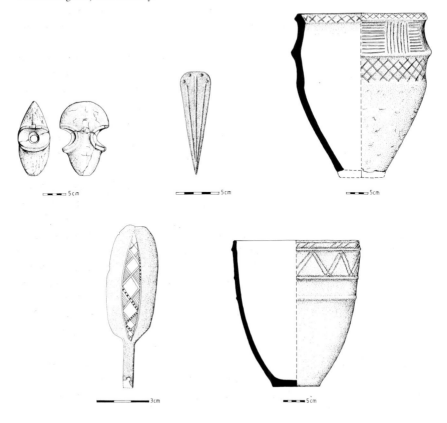

Pygmy Cup, of a kind formerly known as an Incense Cup, which got its name because a few examples had large perforations in their sides which suggested that they contained some sweet-smelling substance. These Pygmy Cups are usually found accompanying Vase Urns or Encrusted Urns, and one example was discovered with an unusual lidded Food Vessel and a bronze dagger at Annaghkeen, Co. Galway. These miniature vessels, rarely more than 6 cm high, are likely to have been a fashion imported from Britain, where they are more commonly found.

The Vase and Encrusted Urns are, in Anna Brindley's view, earlier than the other two major types of Urn in Ireland – the Collared and the Cordoned Urn. The Collared Urn gets its name from the notable collar 64 above its neck. When decorated, the ornament was incised or made with impressed twisted cord, and the motifs in its repertoire included lattice, herring-bone, lozenge, chevron and criss-cross designs. As the name Urn implies, these vessels were generally found with cremation burials, most often in pits, though occasionally in a cist. Other than flint or bone fragments, the two most significant objects found with Collared Urns were the metal dagger and the perforated stone axe-head, both of which were found together in burial 36 in the Mound of the Hostages at Tara in Co. Meath. Collared Urns are found largely in the eastern half of Ireland, whereas the Cordoned Urn, while sharing the same distribution, is found additionally in the midlands and west. The Cordoned Urn is a less decorative affair, having usually two horizontal ribs in relief running around the body of the Urn. Vessels of this kind were mostly buried in pits, as in the Carrowjames cemetery mentioned above. There, they were accompanied by a bronze 'razor' and, like the Collared Urns, they have also been found with a perforated stone axe, as well as with a Pygmy Cup.

The Collared Urns are found much more frequently in England and Wales, and it is probably from there that they were introduced into Ireland. As their strong distribution in northern Ireland corresponds to a similarly dense distribution of Cordoned Urns there, it may well be that the latter type developed in Ulster from the Collared Urns. As both types have been found with Encrusted Urns, there is a likelihood that they were in use at the same time, but the 'razors' found with the Cordoned Urns suggest that the Cordoned Urn may have continued in use until about the fifteenth century bc. How much longer they may have lasted we cannot say, but it would seem likely that Urns accompanying cremations were gradually going out of fashion during the following century or two, after which – for some as yet unexplained reason – we know of very few burials accompanied by gravegoods until the Iron Age. It is at this stage that pottery seems to make its last appearance in the Irish burial record and, with few exceptions, we have to rely on metalwork alone for our knowledge of the archaeology of Ireland for the next 500 years or so.

The foregoing pages have demonstrated a very considerable variety in the form and nature of burial (for example, cist/pit and cremation/

inhumation) and in the shape and decorative motifs of the pottery during the Early Bronze Age in Ireland. Obviously, these variations must have indicated nuances of usage and ritual meaning, but their significance is now beyond our ken. However, the range of burial type and pottery used in the cemetery of Cloghskelt alone (see above) must warn us against reading too much into these variations in terms of population or religious differences. Yet one feature which does emerge is the presence in a few graves of martial gravegoods – daggers and perforated stone axes – suggesting that the Early Bronze Age populations may have been more warlike and therefore, perhaps, under greater territorial and social pressures than their Neolithic antecedents had been.

64

### Settlements

The Cordoned Urn pottery which was placed in graves with the dead, was also apparently used for domestic purposes, as it makes its appearance on settlement sites. Of the ten instances of its probable domestic use recorded in northern Ireland, that at Lough Enagh in Co. Derry had impressions of barley, wheat and oats on the pottery. Of considerable interest too were the finds from Downpatrick, Co. Down, where, beside a once-tidal inlet, Dudley Waterman recovered not only Cordoned Urn pottery, but also the partial plans of two round houses with central hearths, and roofs supported by wooden posts. The diameters of the houses were a little more than 4 m and 7 m respectively. Coney Island in Lough Neagh also produced Cordoned Urn sherds, beneath which was a layer with domestic Bowl pottery and what have been interpreted as rectangular structures with timber posts and sod walls. Both of these structures were about 3 m wide, while one was 6–7 m long and the other more than 3.5 m. The radiocarbon dates for the Downpatrick settlement were c.1845 bc and c.1315 bc, while the Bowl pottery at Coney Island gave a date of c.1400 bc. That Food Vessel pottery was used for domestic as well as funerary purposes is demonstrated not only by the findings at Coney Island, but also at Lough Gur where the houses with Neolithic pottery on Knockadoon also produced Food Vessel sherds, suggesting a continuity into the Early Bronze Age. A roughly square stone house within a circular stone enclosure at Carrigillihy, Co. Cork, was dated by its excavator, Michael J. O'Kelly, to the Early Bronze Age on the basis of crude flat-bottomed pottery and a bronze awl, but it could conceivably be later in date.

13, 14

### Cooking sites

Dudley Waterman considered the possibility that the Cordoned Urn sherds at Downpatrick may have been related to the use of an old Irish cooking place known as a *fulacht fian*. In an undisturbed condition, these cooking places appear as horseshoe or U-shaped mounds, usually placed close to a stream. Two excavated by Michael J. O'Kelly at Killeens, Co.

65

65 Reconstruction of a *fulacht fian* (cooking place) at Ballyvourney, Co. Cork.

Cork, proved to be datable to the second millennium bc, giving dates of *c*.1763 bc and *c*.1556 bc respectively, and Frank Mitchell has obtained comparable radiocarbon dates for others on Valencia Island in Co. Kerry. At Killeens, the centre of one of the horseshoe-shaped mounds was occupied by a rectangular box-like trough, open at the top and made largely of oak planks sunk into the ground. It measured 1.76 by 1.13 m, and was 52 cm deep. The only find was a small fragment of a gold-plated copper ring which came to light beneath the trough.

Experiments which Professor O'Kelly carried out at another similar site at Ballyvourney, nearby, showed that cooking was probably carried on here in the same manner as that described by Geoffrey Keating in his seventeenth-century *History of Ireland*. The trough was first filled with water and then a fire was lit close by. Stones were placed in the fire, and when fully heated, they were thrown into the water-filled trough, which was replenished at intervals with further hot stones until the water boiled.

65

Then a joint of meat, probably wrapped in straw, was placed in the water to boil. Professor O'Kelly's experiments showed that the water could be brought to the boil in thirty to thirty-five minutes, and that hot stones added every few minutes kept the water simmering happily. The time-honoured recipe of twenty minutes to the pound and twenty minutes over proved ample for a 10 lb (4.5 kg) leg of mutton, which emerged well-cooked to the bone after three hours and forty minutes immersion in the hot water. The straw wrapping had kept it free from contamination, so that it turned out to be very tasty by all accounts.

These wooden troughs, and the stones to heat the water they contained, would have been used many times, perhaps hundreds of times over a period of years, and the horseshoe-shaped mound came into being through used stones being thrown up around three sides of the trough – the fourth side being left open for purposes of access. Another such cooking place at Drombeg in Co. Cork provided a radiocarbon date in the Iron Age; the base of the pit was dated to ad 430, and the old ground surface of the cooking pit to ad 560. Indeed, such simple but effective cooking places must have continued in use – though not, of course, necessarily at the same spot – from the second millennium bc probably until the second millennium AD, when the cooking method used must have been sufficiently fresh in people's minds for Geoffrey Keating to have described it so accurately. However, it must be said that Keating's account leaves open the possibility that such sites could also have been used for washing – either of the person, or cloth or hides. The lack of any bones from the joints of meat anywhere in the vicinity can only help to support this latter theory.

### Vegetation, climate and trackways

The copper and bronze axes to be studied below may have been used to clear some of Ireland's forest cover during the second millennium bc. Certainly, the pollen diagrams show a decline in elm and hazel and a corresponding rise in plantain and bracken at this period, suggesting the spread of heath as well as of land available for tillage. The impressions of barley, wheat and oats on the pottery at Lough Enagh give us an indication of the crops cultivated. But it is likely too that at the same time the average temperature was beginning to fall, and a corresponding rise in the annual rainfall may have been responsible for the increase in the number and extent of peat bogs, in which several Bronze Age objects have been found down the years, at depths even exceeding 10 m.

The increase in bog cover in both upland and lowland areas would doubtless have made communication and travel more difficult, and it is significant, therefore, that the earliest known trackway in Ireland dates to the second millennium bc, though earlier examples may yet come to light, as they have in Somerset, England. This Irish trackway was found below 1 m of peat, and stretching for about $\frac{5}{8}$ mile (1 km), in the raised bog at

Corlona, Co. Leitrim. It was built up of planks laid longitudinally and supported by piles. A sample of its timber gave a radiocarbon date of *c*.1440 bc. As this track was only just over 1 m wide, it must have served as a footpath. But another, at Ballyalbanagh in Co. Antrim, was apparently 2.13 m wide. It was built with a foundation of three longitudinal beams of oak set beside one another, on top of which split slabs of oak were placed transversely. George Henry Kinahan, who reported its discovery in 1875, reckoned on the basis of the peat growth above it that it had been constructed in the year 1326 BC. Called toghers, from the Irish word *tóchar*, meaning a causeway, these trackways were to continue to be built in Ireland for thousands of years. Later (Chapter 6) we shall come across 115 another example, discovered more recently, which can be dated by much more precise means exactly to the year 148 BC.

## Copper mines

The same peat which necessitated the building of the trackways almost certainly covered, and thereby ensured for us the preservation of, some of the few prehistoric copper mines known to survive anywhere in Europe outside Austria. They are located on the slopes of Mount Gabriel, near 66 Schull in Co. Cork, and they consist of a total of twenty-five mineshafts in all. Accumulation of water rendered entry to the lower portions of many of them impossible. But the two which the geologist John Jackson was able to examine between 1962 and 1966 had a short narrow access less than 1 m high, which expanded downwards at an angle to the shallow mine proper, which was like a rock-cut room, usually not more than 1.6 m high and 5 m broad. John Deady and Elizabeth Doran examined another with the students of University College, Cork, in 1970, and having drained most of the water, they were able to make a plan and sections of it. On the

66 Plan and cross-section of a Bronze Age mine at Mount Gabriel, Co. Cork.

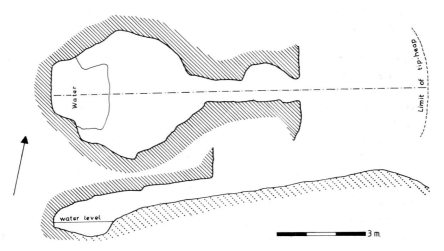

floor of this mine was debris consisting of rock rubble and also mining mauls. These mauls were made from large pebbles, probably found on the beach not very far away, and a number of them had grooves around their widest part for the attachment of rope handles. Once the mineworkers had driven in their adit far enough, they would probably have lit fires as far in as the oxygen would permit. When heated sufficiently by these fires, water thrown onto the mine wall would have shattered them sufficiently for the miners to be able to remove the pieces of ore by means of the stone mauls. These pieces of ore would then have been brought outside where, in front of the mine, the ore would have been separated from the gangue, or waste material. A charcoal sample taken from this waste material, which was found in considerable quantities outside the mine entrances, gave John Jackson a radiocarbon date of *c*.1500 bc. William O'Brien, the most recent investigator of the Mount Gabriel mines, has achieved a slightly later determination of around 1180 bc for wooden tools found within the mine, and another of *c*.1250 bc obtained from a peat sample which was collected from between rock waste in the composite heap outside two of the mines. All of these radiocarbon dates strongly argue against a recent suggestion that the mines are no earlier than the nineteenth century AD. There were, however, mining operations in Cork and Kerry during the last two centuries, including those at Ross Island near Killarney, where mines were opened in 1793–94 by a man named Raspe, who is better known as the author of *The Travels and Adventures of Baron Münchhausen*. There are, however, other old mineworkings in west Cork and Kerry, as well as near Bunmahon, Co. Waterford, which may be of prehistoric date.

John Jackson has estimated that the prehistoric mines of Cork and Kerry produced about 370 tonnes of finished copper, whereas the weight of all the copper and bronze artefacts surviving from the Early Bronze Age in Ireland before 1400 BC is estimated to be a mere 750 kg. From this, he could only conclude that – even if we take account of many bronze objects which still await discovery in the ground, and the much vaster number certainly consigned to the melting pot down the years – Ireland must have exported a considerable amount of copper during the Bronze Age. It is 72, 73 worth noting that only very few of the known Irish moulds, in which Bronze Age objects would have been cast, came from counties Cork or Kerry. This fact may be explained by the slightly old-fashioned notion of itinerant craftsmen travelling with their metal and their moulds throughout the country, making the finished products on the spot where people wanted them, or exchanging the moulds for scrap metal. Alternatively, it may be that copper sources other than those known from Cork and Kerry were used. For copper does occur in other areas of Ireland, including the Rearcross-Silvermines area of north Tipperary mentioned above, though we have no definite proof that it was actually mined during the Bronze Age.

### The first copper, bronze and gold objects

John Jackson's demonstration of the total imbalance between the amount of copper produced from Early Bronze Age mines and the weight of all the artefacts surviving from the period shows just how few of the objects originally cast at the time have survived the 3,000 years down to the present day. Yet even if what does survive be only 1 per cent or less of the material, it nevertheless probably gives us a rough idea of the nature of the original material, as the range of surviving products is really very small. So what was melted down is likely to have been more of the same – but how much more!

What was the fascination of this newly found material, copper, which is considered by archaeologists to have ushered in a new era following the Stone Age, and which caused prospectors to scour the countryside in search of the traces of green malachite and blue azurite which were the tell-tale traces of its presence in the ground or rock-face? Possession of an object made entirely or largely of copper may have given its owner a superiority in society over those who did not possess it. It gave the wielder of a copper or bronze dagger or rapier the edge in any trial of strength, and 80 provided the possessor of a copper or bronze axe with a more reliable and less-breakable implement than a stone one to chop wood or fell forests. Decoration on some of the bronze axe-heads could suggest some magical property perceived to exist in the implement itself which the axe of stone was not considered to possess, while the malleability of the material would have given people a new-found power to mould implements to their own requirements. But even more than copper or bronze, gold, which came 76 into use at about the same time, must have given its wearer an added personal attraction, as it glittered in the sunshine. It could also be seen as a sign of wealth created by the comparative scarcity of the raw material, a status symbol second to none which raised its owner above those other members of society who could not afford to acquire it. Copper, however, was a material available in greater abundance, though control over its mines must have been a prize possession in any early society.

The amount of copper available is reflected in the fact that the Early Bronze Age objects from Ireland consist largely of axes, heavy imple- 67, 68 ments which are not found in anything like the same numbers in England, Scotland or Wales, where the emphasis is on lighter weapons such as daggers, or on ornaments which, in comparative contrast, are much rarer in Ireland – except in gold. It is with the typological development of these daggers and with the axes of copper and bronze that we try to build up the relative succession of the various types of copper and bronze objects in Early Bronze Age Ireland. In doing so, we have to work in something of a vacuum, as many of the individual types are found only with others of the same type. The number of times that these bronze objects are found in association with other – even roughly datable – metal items which would help to create a chronological link between them, is minimal, and few and far between are the instances where bronze and pottery finds can usefully be linked for dating purposes. Even on the rare occasions when a metal dagger is found in a grave with funerary pottery, it is often difficult to relate the dagger to other datable types. We are reduced to a very few associated finds – graves or metalwork hoards – and occasional glimpses across the Irish Sea, in our attempt to establish the development of Irish metalwork of the Earlier Bronze Age.

The most ubiquitous copper object of Early 'Bronze' Age Ireland is the axe, which is invariably found minus its wooden handle with which it would have been wielded to cut down trees – and perhaps the occasional person too. These axes – like many of the individual types of copper and bronze objects – are frequently called after places where one or more typical examples have been found, in order to distinguish one variety from another. The largest group of Irish copper axes – generically termed Type Lough Ravel – are flat, thick-ended and with sides which splay gracefully outwards, as does also the cutting edge. Among this large group, however, Humphrey Case has isolated a smaller grouping centred around a probable hoard from Castletown Roche in Co. Cork, where the sides of the axe tend to be rather more straight. This hoard from Castletown Roche – if such it was – contained just two axes, one with straighter sides and the other with slightly more out-curving sides. That with straighter sides belongs to a type found on the Continent in contexts which are chronologically earlier than the use of Beaker pottery there, while that with more outswinging sides belongs to a type which was found in a hoard at Knocknagur, Co. Galway, with a flat, tanged copper dagger of a type usually associated with Beaker pottery throughout much of Europe.

In the Castletown Roche hoard we have the nub of the problem of the origin of the earliest Irish metallurgy. Were the first Irish copper axes made in a period pre-dating the use of Beaker pottery, possibly by craftsmen coming not from England (where such axes are rare) but rather from France or even as far away as the Iberian Peninsula? Or were the axes made by people who made Beaker pottery? To complicate matters further, analyses of some of these early Irish flat axes have shown them to have been made from *fahlerz*, a slightly grey-coloured copper, the most likely origin of which is considered to be in the southwest of Ireland, though not necessarily the Mount Gabriel mines themselves which – to judge by the radiocarbon dates – are post-Beaker. The distribution map of Beaker pottery, and objects such as tanged metal daggers, V-perforated buttons of jet and archers' wrist guards of stone, as well as barbed-and-tanged arrowheads, show that this whole Beaker 'package' does not seem to have penetrated as far as the southwest, where the copper ore for the axes is likely to have been mined. Unless, in the future, Beaker pottery and the objects associated with it elsewhere, can be found in the southwest to show a stronger connection between Beaker and mining activity, we must leave the question open as to where the earliest Irish copper miners came

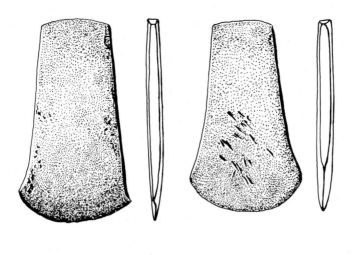

67 Two flat copper axes found together at Castletown Roche, Co. Cork.

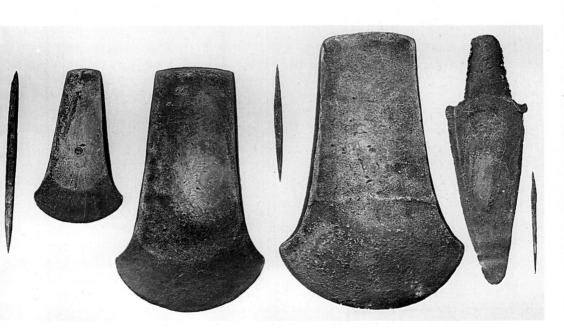

68 Early 'Bronze' Age hoard of copper axe-heads, awls and a tanged dagger (far right) from Knocknagur, Co. Galway.

69 Rock-art on a boulder at Ballynahowbeg, near Cahirciveen, Co. Kerry.

from, and whether it really was the makers of Beaker pottery who introduced metallurgy to Ireland.

It has been suggested, as mentioned earlier, that the builders of stone circles and wedge-tombs may have been associated with early mining in Ireland, as both monument types are found in the copper-bearing areas of west Cork and Kerry. So far, however, no early metal object has been found in association with stone circles or wedges, and as the two groups are also found in areas far away from the known mines or other known copper lodes, and even far from regions where copper and bronze objects have come to light in considerable numbers, the connection must be left as being at best uncertain for the moment. Other unusual stone monuments, not hitherto discussed, have also been seen as having some connection with early metalworking activity. These are what are known as petroglyphs, or natural outcrops of rock or boulders decorated with small hemispherical cupmarks, sometimes surrounded by a circle, which are pocked into the stone surface. Similar markings are found also on stones bearing passage-tomb art, as at Loughcrew, Co. Meath, as well as on standing stones and even on the capstones of Earlier Bronze Age burial cists. The extensive time range hinted at on these man-made monuments show that cupmarks are unlikely to be all contemporary. The parallels which Eoin MacWhite pointed out in the Iberian Peninsula could indicate an Atlantic origin, which is also possible for the earliest flat copper axes. As to the passage-tomb connection, cupmarks do not appear to belong to the 'mainstream' of megalithic art, and as the distribution of cupmarks only rarely corresponds to that of the passage-tombs, too close a connection between the two is preferably avoided. Nevertheless, it ought to be noted that Scotland has produced a number of examples of cupmarks, and it will be remembered that the stone circles of the 'Four Poster' variety are also found there, as they are in Cork. But, as with the stone circles and wedge-tombs, the fact that these cup-and-ring markings also occur in areas unconnected with copper mining, leaves very inconclusive any connection between them and the earliest copper mining. Even if they were to be associated with early metalworking activity, their purpose must remain one of those intriguing and delightful puzzles which will doubtless continue to exercise the mind and imagination of many generations to come.

67
68
71
If we take the Castletown Roche and Lough Ravel/Knocknagur thick-butted axes as the first two stages of development of the copper axe in Ireland, a third stage can be seen in the hoard from Frankford (Birr), Co. Offaly, where the side-view of the axes shows them to have been somewhat thinner at the butt end. As with the earlier two stages, most of the axes of this kind are made of pure copper alloyed with arsenic, though a few have proved on analysis to be of unalloyed copper. This Frankford hoard is of importance because it shows the contemporary use of a more enigmatic object, the copper halberd. This is a blade usually with three heavy metal rivets for the attachment of a wooden handle, of which one

70
intact example was found at Carn in Co. Mayo. This handle gave a radiocarbon date of $c.1050$ bc which, even when calibrated, seems many centuries too late on the basis of current chronology. Some of the halberd blades are curved, others are straight, but most of them have well-cast rounded midribs running roughly parallel with one of the sides. Not many of the halberds – and there are almost 150 examples of this variety known – show any obvious traces of wear, so that it would look as if they were not used for agricultural purposes, such as hoeing, though Michael Ryan suggested that they may have been used as sickles. Perhaps halberds served many purposes, possibly even of a ritual nature, as suggested by the finding of seven examples with their points facing downwards under $2\frac{1}{2}$ ft (0.8 m) of bog at Hillswood, Co. Galway, in 1850. A further hint that they may have played some part in a ritual ceremony, or as the standard borne in front of some important personage, is the halberd held high by a human figure on a rock-carving in Italy, though this could also suggest its

70 Halberd from Carn, Co. Mayo, with its reconstructed wooden handle.

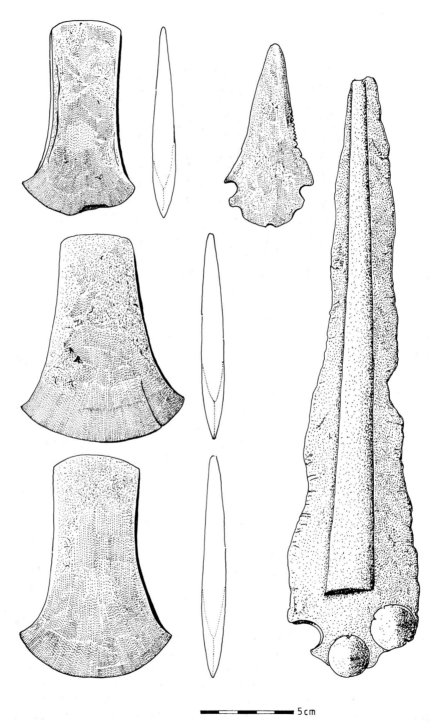

5 cm

71 Hoard of copper axes, dagger and halberd found at Frankford (Birr), Co. Offaly.

72 Irish stone mould for an axe and dagger.

use as a weapon. Italy, the Iberian Peninsula and Central Europe are all possible areas from whence knowledge of the halberd could have come to Ireland, but Ireland is nevertheless the area where this enigmatic object seems to have achieved its greatest popularity, or where the greatest number has survived. The Frankford hoard also included a small riveted dagger which can be paralleled in some late Beaker graves in England, showing that this third stage of metal production corresponds roughly to the period when Beaker pottery was still in use in Ireland.

Axes of the kind found in the Frankford hoard would have been cast in a single, one-piece open stone mould. The shape of the axe would have cf. 73 been hollowed out from the surface of the stone, and into this depression copper or bronze would then have been poured and duly left to cool. Because the bottom of the hollowed-out area is not absolutely flat in the surviving moulds, and the upper surface of the molten metal would have been flat after it had been poured, it is noticeable that some axes cast in these open moulds are slightly asymmetrical when seen from the side, being curved on the side which faced downwards in the mould, and flat on the upper surface, which is sometimes pitted where it was exposed. Sometimes, these stone moulds have matrices for more than one object. Where the matrices are for axes only, it can be seen that the shape of the axe can vary slightly. It is only on the rarest of occasions that a mould will have matrices for two different classes of object, an axe and a dagger, but these are of importance in showing the contemporaneity of the two types 72 of objects.

When the axe was taken out of the mould, it would have been subjected to subsequent hammering, which could obviously result in its shape being slightly altered. Laurence Flanagan has conducted some interesting experiments in trying to match up the shapes of the axe-matrices on the stone moulds to the shapes of the surviving axes. One example shows how 73 an axe from Culfeightrin, Co. Antrim, fits into a mould from Ballynahinch in the neighbouring county of Down. But a stone mould from Ballyglisheen, Co. Carlow, has eight different matrices for axes, and Flanagan has been able to identify a total of twenty-four axes which could have been made in one or other of the Ballyglisheen matrices. Interestingly, not one of these twenty-four axes came from anywhere close to where the mould was found, suggesting that either the moulds and the metal were trundled over widely scattered areas of country for the making of axes wherever they were needed, or that the axes were widely traded from where the craftsman worked from his mould, in the same way 10 that the Neolithic stone axes from Tievebulliagh were extensively traded from the quarry from whence they came in Co. Antrim.

The metal axes and halberds discussed hitherto were made largely of copper with the intentional admixture of arsenic, which makes them stronger and less liable to fracture if they are reworked when cold. But at some stage tin was added to these, and the resulting mixture was bronze, made up of 90 per cent copper and about 10 per cent tin. The tin for the Irish bronze is normally considered to have been imported from Cornwall, but John Jackson has recently made a case for Ireland having had enough native tin to cover the needs of its own bronze industry.

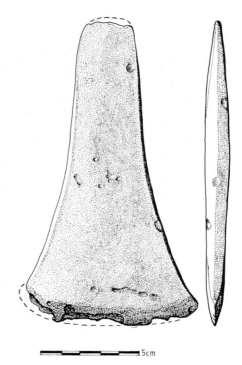

◁73 Axe from Culfeightrin, Co. Antrim, in the matrix of a stone mould from Ballynahinch, Co. Down.

74 A bronze axe of Killaha type from the Beaker settlement at Newgrange, Co. Meath.

5cm

Bronze makes for harder implements which can be more easily hammered than can copper objects while still hot. Humphrey Case maintained that the knowledge of bronze was introduced into Ireland by those who made Beaker pottery, and this suggestion has been greatly strengthened by the finding of a bronze axe in the Beaker settlement at Newgrange. The 74 radiocarbon dates for the settlement there varied, as we have seen, from between *c*.2100 and *c*.1935 bc – so that this Newgrange axe is the first for which we can provide even an approximate date. It also implies, however, that much of the material made of copper – the axes of Castletown Roche 67 and Lough Ravel types, as well as the thin-butted variety found in the Frankford hoard – is likely to be somewhat earlier. But how much earlier, 71 we cannot say. If the makers of Beaker pottery were responsible for both the introduction of metallurgy and the knowledge of bronze in Ireland, then the production of copper axes ought perhaps to be compressed into a period which is only a little more than 200 years before the making of the Newgrange axe, if we see the rise of Beaker pottery as having started around 2150 bc. But if that would seem to have been too short a time, then it would argue more in favour of copper-working having begun in Ireland some time before the making of Beaker pottery, in what was formally a Stone Age society.

The Newgrange axe differs from its copper counterparts in having more obviously splaying sides and, consequently, a larger cutting edge. 74 One similarly shaped example, however, is so large – over 30 cm long and 21 cm wide – that it cannot have been used for practical purposes, and may be regarded as having had some ceremonial or ritual function. The fact

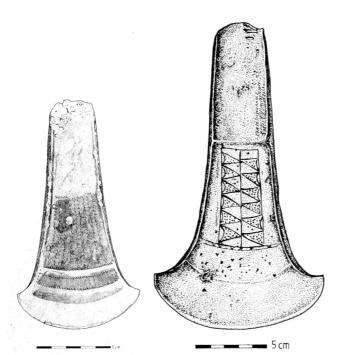

5 cm

5 cm

that a number of Irish axes have been retrieved from rivers, and many more dug out of bogs, could support the notion that they may have been deposited as votive offerings. The Newgrange axe is somewhat similar to a group found in a hoard of bronze objects discovered at Killaha East in Co. Kerry, after which this variety of axe is named. The Killaha East hoard also included a bronze straight-sided halberd of a rare kind with rivets made of a central bronze stem and a conical cap at each end.

A stone mould found at Lyre in Co. Cork had one matrix for an axe of Killaha type and another for a more slender and graceful axe type called Ballyvalley, the most widespread type in Early Bronze Age Ireland. The matrices of the two axes found together on the Lyre mould obviously argues for the two types having been in use at the same time. Nevertheless, an axe similar to the Ballyvalley type was found in a ditch at the southern English henge at Mount Pleasant in Dorset, where the radiocarbon date was *c.*1778 bc, which would indicate either a later date or a longer duration for the use of the Ballyvalley axes. This Mount Pleasant axe bears decoration hammered in to look like a lot of raindrops. Decoration is also a feature of many of the Irish Ballyvalley axes where, in cf. 75   addition to the shower of raindrops, motifs such as zigzags and hatched triangles are found. As the Mount Pleasant example shows, axes of this kind, including some bearing decoration, have also been found in England, where they may represent a local analogy to, or even imitation of, this popular Irish axe form. Further specimens have come to light in Denmark, where they could conceivably have been imported from Ireland, or have been made by some hypothetical travelling Irish bronzesmith.

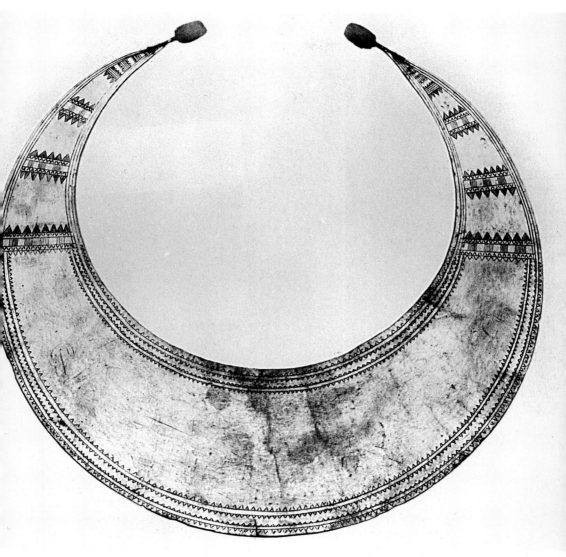

There is another type of object of a very different material which also bears the geometrical ornament of the kind found on some of the Ballyvalley axes. This is the gold lunula, which gets its name from its half-moon shape, and it is likely that it was worn as a neck ornament, though none has ever been found on a skeleton to prove it. The decoration of the gold lunulae consists mostly of combinations of lines, zigzags and hatched triangles incised into the surface of this malleable material. The decoration on the lunulae suggests that they may have been made at about the same time as the Ballyvalley axes, and possibly also the Killaha axes, a few of which bear decoration. These lunulae are made of thin, hammered sheets of gold.

76

74, 75

77 Possibly slightly earlier in date are round 'sun-discs', small rounded sheets of gold sometimes found in pairs and usually having two small central perforations indicating that they were probably sewn onto garments and used therefore as jewellery – the purpose of almost all of the many gold objects known from Bronze Age Ireland. The sun-discs, often decorated with a cross-shaped motif, hammered up in repoussé technique from the back, are also known from Beaker contexts in southern England. The Irish sun-discs were made of gold from the same source as that used in the lunulae. Dr Axel Hartmann, of Stuttgart, examined the Irish gold objects and found that the composition of the sun-disc and lunula gold was comparable to that from a natural gold nugget found in the area of Croghan Kinshelagh in Co. Wicklow in the eighteenth century, and he presumed therefore that the sun-discs and lunulae were made of gold washed from the Goldmines and other rivers of Co. Wicklow. But the other Irish gold objects which he analyzed were found to be of a gold with a different composition. Because he presumed – wrongly – that Wicklow was the only source of gold in Ireland, he further presumed that all the Irish gold jewellery other than sun-discs and lunulae must have been made of a gold imported from outside Ireland, without being able to locate any actual source. But, as we shall see in the next chapter, Ireland was so rich in gold objects in the Later Bronze Age, that it seems much more likely that they were made from gold found either elsewhere in Wicklow or in some other parts of Ireland where the gold supply from rivers has long been exhausted. Certainly, in areas like the Sperrin Mountains of Co. Tyrone, it is quite likely that more gold would have been available in prehistoric times than can be found in rivers today and, until such time as a precise source for the non-lunula gold can be located outside Ireland, it would seem preferable on general grounds to assume that the great majority of the Bronze Age gold objects from Ireland were made from Irish gold. Lunulae have also been found in Britain and on the Continent, but they were not necessarily made in Ireland.

75, 76 With the lunulae and the Ballyvalley axes, Ireland reached the zenith of its metal production in the earlier part of the Bronze Age. Subsequently, the axes – while still continuing to be decorated – become fewer in number and smaller in size, and the numbers of hoards containing axes becomes drastically reduced for reasons which have not yet been satisfactorily explained. The shapes of the axes now seem to have been increasingly dictated by fashions current in England where the prosperity of the wealthy merchant princes in Wessex was beginning its decline around the fifteenth century BC. Irish daggers of the time, still few in number but becoming longer and developing curving blades, also seem to be aping English models, so much so that the impression is created that the Irish bronze industry was losing its individuality, and was being surpassed by an increasing bronze production in England which, in turn, was closely following in the footsteps of recent developments on the

77 Gold 'sun-disc' from Tedavnet, Co. Monaghan.

78 Decorated bronze axe-head found together with its leather sheath and thong at Brockagh, Co. Kildare.

79 Irish bronze spearhead with loops on the socket for attachment.

5 cm

Continent. At the same time, however, it is clear that new methods of warfare were being practised, for it is the period around the fifteenth century BC which saw both in England and in Ireland the introduction of
79 the spearhead, with loops on the socket for attachment.

The appearance of the spearhead was also the reflection of newly developed casting techniques, such as core-casting, which enabled a hollow socket to be made for the wooden spear-shaft. This would scarcely have been possible without the use of the twin-valve mould, whereby the matrix for one half of the object would have been hollowed out on the faces of two separate but identical stone moulds which would then be fitted together. One such mould came from Inch Island in Co. Donegal, and it bore matrices not only for spearheads but also for an object known as a 'trunnion chisel'. Such twin-valve moulds were also used for the making of axes, so that it now became possible to cast axes with raised flanges on the sides and transverse ribs across their faces in order to prevent them from slipping in their forked wooden handles. These axes, which have straight sides and frequently bear decoration, are noticeably smaller than those of the preceding stages, but they compensate for this by having a wide, almost semicircular, cutting edge. The bronze 'razors' found in the
64 Urn cemetery at Pollacurragune, mentioned earlier, may – on the basis of English parallels – be datable to the same stage, thus showing us that Urn burial was still being practised at the time, say around 1450–1250 bc, or

about 1400 BC, at the latest. To this stage, too, we would expect some of the daggers with curved blades to belong, of the kind made in the fine mould from Inchnagree, Co. Cork. But gradually these daggers lengthened into rapiers, so as to enable the user to thrust at enemies from a greater distance. One example, from Lissane, Co. Derry, a real *tour-de-force* in the art of casting, reached the impressive length of 79.7 cm. At the same time, there was a noticeable development in the height of the flanges on the axes and the strength of their cross-ribs, and there was even a novel form of implement, the palstave, which was probably introduced along with a new lead-bronze alloy and the use of clay in making two-piece moulds.

A wind of change in the bronze industry in Ireland after 1200 BC can be felt in an important hoard from Bishopsland, Co. Kildare, which presents us with the hidden baggage of a travelling smith of the period. He had buried his anvil and vice, as well as a saw, in the vain hope of recovering them. Perhaps as his stock in trade of saleable objects he carried with him not only some older-fashioned items such as the 'trunnion chisel' and the palstave, but also some newer 'lines' – the socketed axe-head and chisel, which were to remain in vogue for centuries, and which may have been ultimately of German/Baltic origin. Another more recent invention which he was carrying with him was the bronze sickle which, however, in this case, had no socket to attach it to its handle. Although the smith did not deposit any moulds with his tools, he would probably have used twin-valve clay moulds to make many of the objects. One rough contemporary of the man who concealed this Bishopsland hoard was not an itinerant smith, as he was, but a sedentary craftsman working in his small workshop at Lough Gur in Co. Limerick, where broken moulds for casting spearheads, rapiers and palstaves came to light in a house. Prehistory is silent as to why the Bishopsland smith felt obliged to bury his tools and his other metal possessions, but it is clear that Bishopsland is only one of a number of hoards deposited around the twelfth century BC. This documents a revival of the old hoard-burying custom which had been common up to about three centuries before that, and which could indicate – among other things – the advent of a period of unrest at the time.

What is probably another hoard of the period was found at Annesborough, Co. Armagh, in 1913. In it was not only a palstave, but also bronze ornaments, including a twisted bronze bracelet. It is indeed characteristic that almost all the hoards of the last few centuries of the second millennium BC testify to an upsurge in the use of personal ornaments. It was then that the goldsmith once more came into his own, presumably because of the greater availability of the metal, for many of the ornaments datable to this period are made of bar gold, more solid than the sheet gold of the lunulae and 'sun-discs'. The gold was panned from streams which have not yet been satisfactorily identified, but what is noticeable is the addition of a copper alloy in the gold. Some of the earliest

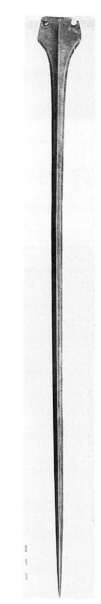

80 A beautifully slender bronze rapier-blade dating from shortly before 1200 BC. The surviving rivet and its fellow, which has disappeared, attached it to a wooden grip.

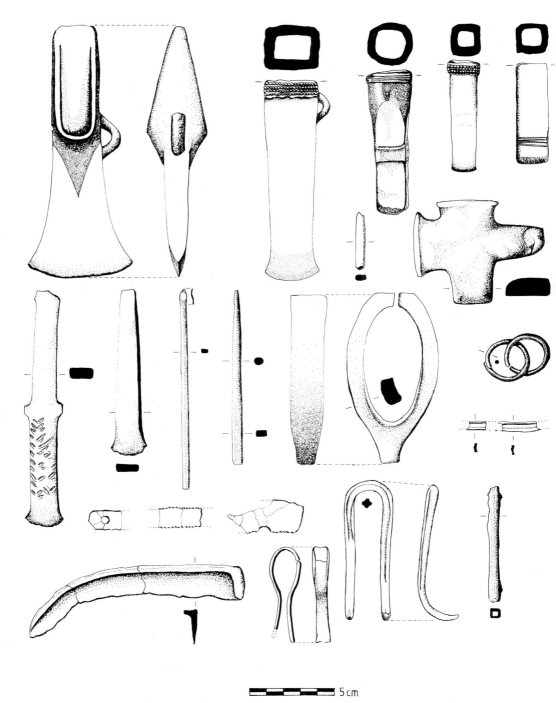

81 A hoard of bronze weapons and tools from Bishopsland, Co. Kildare, perhaps the hidden baggage of a travelling smith. Among the items are axe-heads, chisels, an anvil and a sickle.

gold objects of this period are small in size, such as the earrings, but they    82
betray the introduction of new techniques, for instance twisting the body
of a large piece of gold wire – imitations of more complicated Oriental    83
fabrications which the western goldsmiths could not copy satisfactorily.
This new twisting of the gold was practised in a variety of ways on much
larger bracelets, as well as on neck and body ornaments, known as torcs.
These may have been modelled on bronze ornaments such as the one in
the Annesborough hoard, but the bronze prototypes are most likely to
have come to Ireland from Northern Europe (where gold was scarce), via
southern England, and it is quite possible that the Annesborough torc is,
in fact, an import from southern England. The great gold bar-torcs with
recurved terminals are 'among the most elaborate types of ornament
found in Bronze Age Europe' in the words of George Eogan, and they
were produced by craftsmen who were unequalled anywhere in Europe at
the time.

Another unusual type which makes its appearance at this time is the
gold bracelet, such as that found at Derrinboy, Co. Offaly, which is    84
decorated with repoussé ornament. This new-found joy in personal
adornment may have resulted in the search for and discovery of additional
gold sources. The use of the pin as an ornament might also suggest the
introduction of a new form of garment which it could have helped to
fasten. This peacock-like but not too ostentatious fashion in showing off
one's gold jewellery is, however, also a reflection of fashions common in
the 'ornament' horizon of southern Britain in the twelfth century BC,
though some of the metal implements show close connections also with
Northern and Western continental Europe. It would be unwise to
speculate on new techniques in the metal industry as indicating signs of
folk movements, other than the possible arrival of a handful of bronze and
goldsmiths – possibly exploiting anew the Wicklow gold, as most of the
hoards of the period are found not too far away from the gold-bearing
Wicklow hills. They may have been not just smiths and metal-seekers, but
also traders as well, for some of the bar-torcs found in Britain were
perhaps manufactured in Ireland, and the gold from which they were
made came in all probability from Ireland too.

The vigorous industry which began to flourish in the period around
1200 BC, and which is most easily exemplified in the Bishopsland hoard, is
one which was not anticipated in the immediately preceding centuries. It
introduces a freshness into a long-established traditional industry, a
novelty which comes doubtless largely from southern English stimulus.
The gold would suggest a rise in the wealth of certain elements of the
population, and the innovations which the smiths brought about were to
continue to have a lasting effect for centuries. Indeed, they were
eventually to be instrumental in the start of a tradition which later became
one of the most productive periods in Irish metalworking during the first
half of the first millennium BC, which is the subject of the ensuing chapter.

82–84 **Irish craftsmanship in gold** (*Right*)
Flanged gold earring from Castlerea,
Co. Roscommon. (*Centre*) Detail of the
flanged gold torc from Tara, Co. Meath. Its
maximum diameter is 38 cm. (*Bottom*)
Ribbed gold bracelet from a hoard found at
Derrinboy, Co. Offaly.

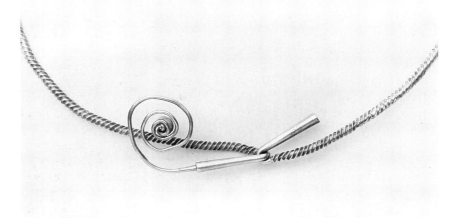

# 5·A Golden Age

### Swords, horns, shields and cauldrons

IN THE ABSENCE of burials or settlements to illuminate our story, metalwork is the only – and tenuous – link between the Earlier and Later Bronze Ages, the latter commencing *c.*1000 BC. From the technological developments and advancements in bronze and goldworking, we try in vain to fill out the political and social history in the 600 years from, say, 1400 to 800 BC. This was the period which saw the movement southwards into the eastern Mediterranean of barbarian hordes which contributed to the downfall of those great Bronze Age powers, the Hittite empire and Mycenae. For centuries, Europe turned its back on the Mediterranean which was unable to offer it much until the rise of the Phoenicians and their burgeoning rivals in pre-classical Greece. Yet the unrest which led to the lights going out over much of the Mediterranean was counterbalanced by an *aurora borealis*, the metallic glisten from the products of a Central and more northerly European gold and bronze industry which developed in a splendid – if not entirely complete – isolation of its own. The Mediterranean's Dorian doldrums may somehow be related to the turmoil which we see through a glass darkly in the Urnfield peoples of much of Central Europe, an unrest which makes its presence felt in southern Britain around the turn of the millennium with the introduction of the bronze sword – a development which seems to have come about only after the deposition of the Bishopsland hoard. 81 The new weapon, used more for slashing combat than the thrusting rapier, was not long in making inroads from the Thames through south Wales to Ireland, where it developed into swords of the Ballintober type. Their makers, whatever about their wielders, seem to be connected with the smiths who deposited hoards like that from Bishopsland some time before the end of the second millennium, and who continued to make traditional items such as rapiers, spearheads and palstaves, while at the same time introducing socketed implements and a considerable variety of gold ornaments. Despite the growing popularity of the sword, the metalworking traditions of the Bishopsland hoard and other roughly contemporary items seem to have continued for hundreds of years until the advent of what can only be described as an 'industrial revolution' around the eighth century BC. This manifests itself in an astonishing increase in the amount of metal available, with lead often added to the already ubiquitous bronze to make it more fluid in casting. Hand in hand comes the appearance of a multiplicity of ranges of objects showing a high technical quality in their manufacture, doubtless partially inspired and assisted by a network of connections with other parts of Europe. The eighth and seventh centuries BC must indeed be regarded as one of the great highlights of prehistoric Ireland.

These centuries also experienced the deposition of a remarkable number of hoards. Many of these have been found during the last two centuries in bogs or close to water, strongly suggesting something of a water cult to appease the weather gods at a time when climatic conditions may have been deteriorating. It is not often easy to decide whether any group of objects found together were placed in the ground as a hoard – to avoid capture perhaps in a time of social unrest – or as a votive deposit, to honour the cult of some god or chthonic power. This problem of interpretation faces us when we come to consider the Dowris 'hoard', found probably in boggy terrain between two midland lakes in Co. Offaly during the 1820s and which, because of its richness and the variety of its material, has given its name to this most productive phase of Irish prehistory around the eighth and seventh centuries BC. The slightly conflicting reports of the find do not make it absolutely clear whether the objects – totalling over 200 – were all found together. At least 185 of the original items can be identified, and although these include a few scraps of waste bronze metal which could suggest that this was the hurriedly hidden property of some itinerant bronzesmith, the large number of rather unusual objects and their burial in a bog could well speak more in favour of a ritual deposit, though sadly the veil is drawn as much over the reasons for its original deposition as it was over the circumstances of its discovery. Because the Dowris find sums up so many facets of Irish bronze production in the period around 700 BC, it is worthwhile to take a closer look at its contents.

The Dowris find included five swords, most of them related to similar weapons in the south of England. All but one of the spearheads are of a slightly old-fashioned, leaf-shaped outline, the exception – which has a lunate opening in the blade – being perhaps a more recent invention. The axe-heads, socketed for easier hafting, are typical of this period in Britain and Ireland, though the inspiration for those from Dowris may have come ultimately from northern Germany, with Britain acting as an inter-mediate station. Further tools included gouges, chisels and knives, which would have been used by a woodworker of the period. The find also contained objects identified, somewhat uncertainly, as razors. The most numerous items were also the most enigmatic of all. Called 'crotals', they may have been tradesmens' weights, though the resemblance of their shape to a bull's scrotum has led John Coles to postulate their purpose as being related to a European fertility cult connected with the bull. With this cult he also associated the Irish bronze horns, as these must ultimately have been modelled on the bull's horns. These horns, of which twenty-six survived at Dowris, can be either straight, or curved, and some have

85

cf. 86

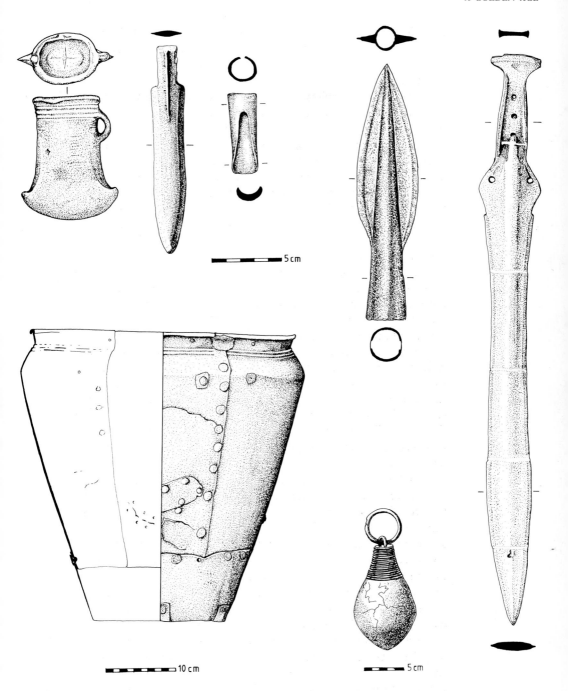

85 A selection of the many objects found at Dowris, Co. Offaly, clockwise from top left: socketed axe, tanged knife, gouge, spearhead, sword, 'crotal' and Kurd-type bucket. (Ht of spearhead, 19 cm; sword, 42 cm.)

135

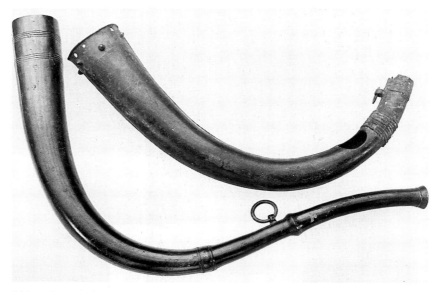

86 Late Bronze Age horns from Chute Hall, Co. Kerry (top) and Dromabest, Co. Antrim.

conical spikes placed near the bell or non-playing end. The horns were blown either from the side or the end, depending upon where the maker placed the blow-hole. Recent experiments have shown that even without a mouthpiece – which none of the Irish specimens has – the horns are capable of producing a wide variety of sound characteristic of the modern Australian Aborigine instrument known as a *didjeridu*.

The horns were ingeniously cast in two-piece moulds, showing a high degree of technical mastery. But the Dowris 'hoard' also contained vessels made of individual bronze sheets riveted together. One of these is a bucket which, despite its prosaic name, is perhaps the most intriguing item in the whole assemblage because, as Christopher Hawkes and M.A. Smith showed so convincingly, it was imported from an area of Eastern Central Europe around the eighth century B C. Although there is no evidence from Dowris to prove it, it is quite possible that such a bucket may have been a particularly important cult object placed upon a miniature waggon, which could have been drawn in procession by a horse, to which discs known as phalerae and also rattle-pendants may have belonged. Dowris itself also contained fragments of other buckets, which may have been local copies of the imported bucket, while a fine complete local imitation, decorated
87 with ornament in repoussé technique, was found in Capecastle bog in Co. Antrim.

The other type of sheet-bronze vessel found at Dowris was the cauldron, of which one complete example and a handle survive. The Late

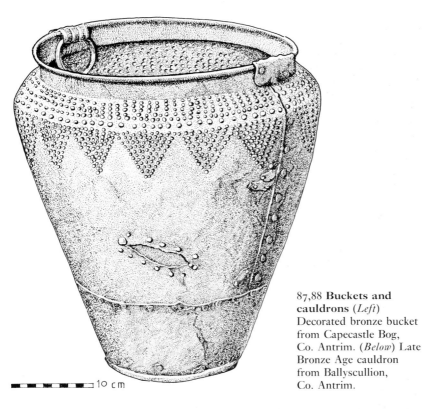

10 cm

87,88 **Buckets and cauldrons** (*Left*) Decorated bronze bucket from Capecastle Bog, Co. Antrim. (*Below*) Late Bronze Age cauldron from Ballyscullion, Co. Antrim.

89 Bronze fleshhook adorned with water-birds, from Dunaverney, Co. Antrim. It was used to take meat from a cauldron, such as that illustrated in ill. 88.

cf. 88 Bronze Age cauldrons of Ireland come in two varieties, one with a short upright neck and the other with a rim everted at a slant, and both varieties appear to be represented at Dowris. The prototypes of these cauldrons probably came from the Mediterranean, passing through the hands of Greek and possibly also Phoenician traders. Examples found in France and northern Spain suggest that they may have come to Ireland across southern France and then northwards up the Atlantic coast trade-route, though a Central European origin – like that of the buckets – must also be kept in mind as a possibility. Again it was Hawkes and Smith who showed that the Dowris cauldrons probably belonged to the first half of the seventh century BC, the period when the objects are likely to have been deposited at Dowris, but it is also possible that the imported bucket was half a century old when consigned to mother earth. In old Irish mythology, cauldrons played an important role as an attribute of abundance associated with the good god Dagda and, in the minds of those who created the tales, supernatural banquet-halls were supplied with such cauldrons. It is not unreasonable to imagine these bronze cauldrons, or their Iron Age successors, as being not only the models for the teller of mythological tales but also a centrepiece of some great ritual feast of the time. The cauldrons had two great rings so that they could be suspended from a stout pole and thus carried into the feast, fully laden, on the shoulders of two sturdy attenders, perhaps accompanied by the deep sounds emanating from the horns. Meat in the cauldron would have been

89 taken out with a fleshhook, like that found at Dunaverney in Co. Antrim. Certainly the indications from the bucket, the horns and the cauldrons are that the Dowris 'hoard' had a strong ritual element to it – and many if not all the objects from the find would appear to have been discovered lying in the cauldron.

One important type of sheet-bronze object which did not form part of
90–93 the Dowris find is the shield, of which only a handful have survived in Ireland, in comparison with the much greater number known from England. Of the two differing varieties of shield, one – exemplified by that
91 found at Athenry in Co. Galway – has a large central boss covering the

handle for holding the shield on the inside, and outside the central boss there are either two concentric circles of bosses of different sizes, or simply four bosses in cross formation. These shields vary in size – from 27 to 35 cm in diameter – so small that they may not have offered a warrior much protection in battle, and this has given rise to the theory that they may have had a largely ceremonial use. The fact that the find circumstances of the Irish shields, where known, are associated with bogs or water – a river or a lake – can only lend support to the notion of their having had some ritual nature.

The second variety of shield, to which one found at Lough Gur 90 belongs, has a multiple series of concentrically arranged small bosses around a single large central boss, which represents a masterly piece of casting. The parallels for this variety of Irish shield can be found in southern England, northern Germany or Scandinavia. Because the gap between the rim and the outer circle of bosses is not found on English shields, but is present on those known from Scandinavia, it is more likely that it is from the latter area that Ireland got its inspiration for these shields. But as the shields are much more numerous outside Ireland, it would appear that the same importance was not attached to the shield in Ireland as was the case in Britain or Scandinavia.

However, the Irish bogs have helped to preserve wooden and leather shields not known elsewhere, which demonstrates that Ireland may have known far more shields than the surviving bronze examples would lead one to believe. Leather shields may not seem to provide much protection, but practical experiments have shown that they are surprisingly strong and resistant, much more so indeed than the bronze variety which can be shattered by a single sword slash. Together with the surviving Irish wooden examples, they show one interesting feature not present on any of the Irish bronze shields. This is a V- or U-shaped notch on one side. Shields with V-shaped notches are known from Greece and the Iberian Peninsula, whereas the U-shaped notches are a predominantly Nordic characteristic, so that the Irish may have been getting ideas for their war-gear from both of these areas, and it is interesting that neither variety of notch is present on any of the English shields. But that a trade in weapons could also go in the opposite direction is shown by some spearheads of possible Irish manufacture which were found in a hoard – probably the wreck of a trader's ship – discovered in the river Huelva in southwestern Spain. Two of the Irish wooden shields, now buckled from their originally circular shape, were probably actual wooden shields. These are the specimens from Annandale, Co. Leitrim and Cloonlara, Co. Mayo. 92 The others – from Churchfield, Co. Mayo and Kilmahamogue, Co. Antrim – are more likely to have been moulds for the making of leather shields like the one from Clonbrin, Co. Longford, whereby the leather 93 shield would have been spread in a wet state over the mould, and then hammered into it.

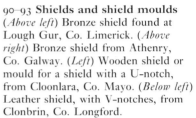

**90–93 Shields and shield moulds**
(*Above left*) Bronze shield found at
Lough Gur, Co. Limerick. (*Above
right*) Bronze shield from Athenry,
Co. Galway. (*Left*) Wooden shield or
mould for a shield with a U-notch,
from Cloonlara, Co. Mayo. (*Below left*)
Leather shield, with V-notches, from
Clonbrin, Co. Longford.

## Goldwork: the glory of ancient Ireland

Together with the horns and cauldrons, the greatest glory of Ireland's Late Bronze Age is undoubtedly its goldwork, of which the country has an astounding collection, although Hartmann would insist that the gold which went into its making was not of Irish origin. Symptomatic of this richness is what is known as the 'great Clare find', a hoard of 146 gold objects found close to the hillfort of Mooghaun North in Co. Clare, when the narrow-gauge West Clare railway (now sadly defunct) was being constructed in 1854. George Eogan claims that it is by far the largest associated find of gold objects of Bronze Age date from anywhere in Europe outside the Aegean. Sadly, many of the pieces were melted down not long after their discovery, though not before casts were made which are now displayed in the National Museum in Dublin. The hoard contained three main types of ornament – collars, penannular neckrings and penannular bracelets with expanded terminals, the last category of which made up the vast majority of the objects found. Only the collars bore incised ornament, consisting of hatched triangles and herring-bone motifs. The penannular bracelets have expanding terminals of various sizes. Other similar examples found elsewhere also have expanding terminals but much shorter bows, as seen on that from Clones in Co. Monaghan, which bears ornament of concentric circles. These have been dubbed 'dress-fasteners' because it is presumed that the expanded ends

94

95

94 Gold ornaments from the 'great Clare find'.

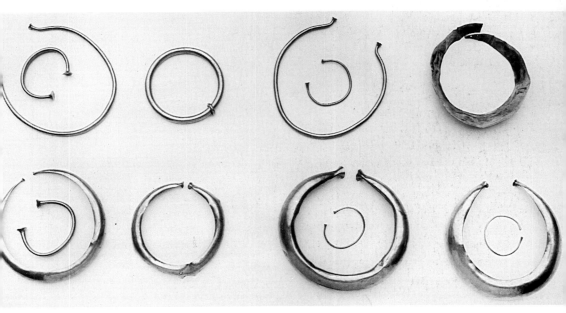

fitted into buttonhole-like slits to hold the two sides of a cloak together. Christopher Hawkes has suggested that the shape was adapted from safety-pins or fibulae of a kind known in Northern Europe, and it is interesting that an Irish example was found at Gahlstorf, near Bremen, in northern Germany, brought there probably on a trade-route across Scotland. But some of these 'dress-fasteners' are made of such massive gold that they would have been an awesome weight to wear, so that the decorated examples – such as that from Clones – may have been worn only on ceremonial occasions. Those without any ornament may conceivably never have been worn at all, but may have served as a kind of 'money', or as ingots for the making of other gold objects.

94     The 'great Clare find' is only one of the many testimonies to the great richness of gold ornaments of the eighth and seventh centuries BC which have come from the counties bordering the lower reaches of the river Shannon. But as there are no obvious local sources for the gold, this richness has been variously explained as evidence for a possible trading depot or even the incursion of foreign goldsmiths who set up workshops there. Another interesting Co. Clare hoard is that from Gorteenreagh, which introduces us to a different group of gold ornaments found along with penannular bracelets like those in the great Clare find. The most eye-catching of these is the gorget. However, because the Gorteenreagh

96     gorget is damaged, another example – from Gleninsheen, also in Co. Clare – is illustrated here to show what it was like when fully assembled. The gorget, probably a neck ornament, is of more sophisticated construction than the earlier lunulae which probably also served the same purpose.

95,96 **Gold jewellery** (*Below*) Gold 'dress-fastener' from Clones, Co. Monaghan. (*Opposite*) Gold gorget of the Late Bronze Age found at Gleninsheen, Co. Clare.

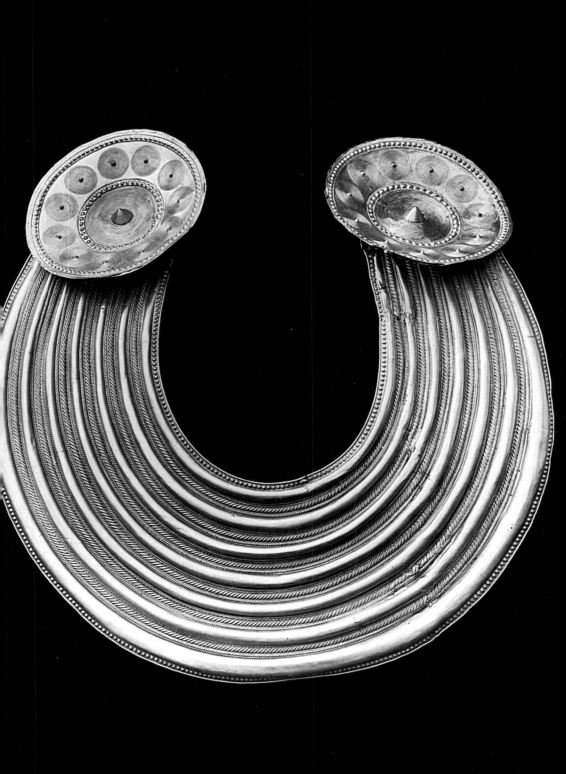

97 Detail of the gold gorget from Ardcrony, Co. Tipperary.

The main body of the gorget consists of the curved part having rounded and roughly concentric ridges with rope ornament in between, all hammered up from the back in repoussé technique, even though they may look as if they were hammered onto a wooden mould. Attached to both narrow ends, usually by means of thin gold wire, there is a disc consisting of two disc-shaped pieces joined at the edges, of which the outer one is decorated with concentric circles having a conical spike at the centre. The spike, like those of bronze found on some of the horns and cauldrons, is

98 Fragment of Late Bronze Age tasselled ornament made from horse-hair, found with remains of cloth and bronze objects at Cromaghs, Co. Antrim.

considered to have been borrowed from Nordic bronzesmiths, who probably also provided the inspiration for the concentric circular ornament, and possibly also the models for the series of ribbed ornaments. But Terence Powell argued that the discs may be a reflection of the flower ornaments found on Phoenician jewellery, and that the cable or rope decoration between the ribs may be an Irish adaptation of the minuscule granulation known in the Mediterranean world, but which the Irish craftsmen were unable to copy. The Irish gorgets may, therefore, be seen as combining the ideas of smiths from areas as far apart as the Mediterranean and the Baltic.

It may be mentioned here that the ornamentation of concentric circles is also found chased on a beautifully executed disc found with gold penannular bracelets at Lattoon, Co. Cavan, as well as on closed gold boxes such as that from Ballinclemesig, Co. Kerry, where the circular decoration has been hammered up from the back. It also occurs on disc-headed pins which seem to have formed an important method of fastening clothes in the Late Bronze Age, though toggles – as provided on duffle-coats today – would have been in use too. Garments may also have been belted at the time, as a piece of worn horsehair with ornamental tassels found at Cromaghs, Co. Antrim, seems to have functioned as a belt. Both 98 the pins and the toggles are apparently of Nordic inspiration, and it is not impossible that some of the toggles which have survived in Ireland may actually have been imported from Scandinavia.

99 Two superb gold 'lock-rings' from a hoard found at Gorteenreagh, Co. Clare.

The Gorteenreagh hoard also has other gold objects of interest. One of these is the so-called 'sleeve-fastener', in which discs are joined by a small, and often striated, arched bow. Such 'sleeve-fasteners', of which about seventy are known from Ireland, would have functioned much like cuff-links do today, but in the Late Bronze Age they would probably have served to link two parts of some garment which might have been of a thinner material than the cloaks which we presume were fastened by the heavier 'dress-fasteners'. But technically a much greater masterpiece is the 'lock-ring' found at Gorteenreagh, of a kind usually taken to have been used as hair ornaments. These 'lock-rings' consist of a central tube and two conical shapes, complete except for a small slit into which the locks of hair may have fitted. The cones are decorated with minute concentric lines which, at first sight, would appear to have been incised. But microscopic examination has shown that the lines are made up of minute wires about 0.33 mm wide. The incredible feat of making these tiny wires and placing them so perfectly alongside one another, something which even modern jewellers would find it hard to emulate, almost seems to foreshadow the love of miniature-scale ornament which the painters of the Book of Kells were to execute a millennium and a half later.

Because it is used almost entirely for jewellery, gold was obviously a highly prized metal in Late Bronze Age Ireland, and the amount of gold objects which have survived from the period demonstrates what great quantities must have been available. But why so much of it was,

99

or had to be, confined to the earth, as in the case of the 'great
Clare find', can only be the subject of speculation. Were the goldsmiths, 94
or the objects' owners, threatened by some impending catastrophe which
would leave them hungry after a number of bad harvests – or dead
through some disease of epidemic proportions? The apparently ritual
nature of the deposition of the bronze Dowris 'hoard' cannot reasonably 85
be invoked for most of the hoards of gold objects – with one or two
exceptions. The Bog of Cullen in north Tipperary, for instance, which
was exploited for its peat in the eighteenth and nineteenth centuries,
produced over the years a total of around 100 known gold objects,
including at least one gold vessel which has since been melted down, along
with all the other pieces from the same bog. The fact that they were not all
found at the same time creates the impression that they were scattered in
the bog, and perhaps offered on a number of separate occasions to appease
some important deity.

The rich treasury of some of the gold types just discussed are, in many
cases, concentrated in the northern part of the modern province of
Munster, and this is particularly the case with the 'lock-rings' and the 99
gorgets, as well as with the gold boxes and other vessels, though it also 96, 97
includes one of the varieties of bronze horns mentioned above. George cf. 86
Eogan has pointed out how this contrasts with the distribution of 'sleeve-
fasteners', the bronze buckets, one of the varieties of cauldrons and the 87, 88
other variety of bronze horns, which are largely confined to the northern
half of Ireland – the Dowris find being the one point where the differing
distributions of bronze objects meet. While underlining thereby the
significance of the Dowris 'hoard' as that of a possible central sacrificial 85
site, it also brings out the different tastes prevalent in the northern and
southern halves of the country in the Late Bronze Age. It may also hint at
some more deep-rooted division of the population which we can only
guess at, but which seems to cast its shadow forward to developments in
the Iron Age to be discussed in the next chapter.

## Contacts overseas

The many signs of Nordic influence on the decoration and shapes of gold
jewellery, and other objects of the eighth and the first half of the seventh
century BC, in Ireland, were possibly an exchange for the bronze and
perhaps also the gold which, like the Gahlstorf 'dress-fastener', Ireland
may have been exporting at the period to the peoples of northern
Germany and Scandinavia, who had been cut off from their traditional
metal sources in the Carpathians. The Dowris bucket is an import from
eastern Central Europe, and England must have played a role in passing it
and other continental innovations to Ireland. The cauldrons and V-
notched shields suggest a derivation from the Mediterranean, probably
across the south of France and then up the Atlantic coast, while the
spearheads from Huelva are visible proof of a trade in the direction of the

south of Spain. All of these show that Irish craftsmen were able to respond brilliantly in their own way to outside stimuli coming from various quarters, making their own highly individual products by assimilating ideas borrowed from elsewhere.

But in the latter part of the seventh century BC, the impetus from outside both changes and declines. The change was brought about by the arrival of influences from the rising power of what are known as the Hallstatt C cultures in Central Europe. The most obvious visual sign of this is the so-called Gündlingen sword, the idea for which reached Ireland from the Continent through Britain. Over forty Irish swords of this type are known, though this number is small in comparison to the 400 swords of Ballintober type which have been discovered. These swords are made of a bronze with a reduced lead content, and they have a very distinctive boat-shaped or winged chape at the foot of their scabbards. George Eogan has identified a bracelet with bulbous ends in a hoard from Kilmurry, Co. Kerry, as another example of Hallstatt C influence, and Hawkes has suggested that the great increase in the deposition of hoards with material of Dowris type may have been signals of a people who felt alarmed and threatened by the arrival of new sword-bearers of Hallstatt type from the Continent. There are also specific types of socketed axes which may also represent imports of the same period, though it is interesting to note the survival of the older, indigenous type down to later centuries, as

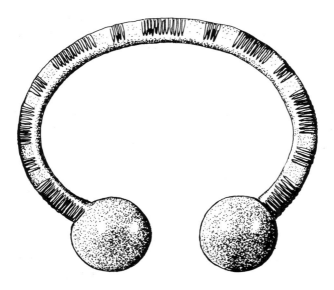

100 Bronze bracelet
from Kilmurry,
Co. Kerry.

3 cm

evidenced by the recent radiocarbon date of $c.170$ bc for a socketed axe found in an excavation at Kilsmullan, Co. Fermanagh. This date, which must however be treated with some caution, indicates the considerable difficulty in finding out how long the bronze industry represented by the Dowris 'hoard' may have continued. For while it may have lasted for some considerable time, possibly even centuries, after 600 BC we have very little evidence to show the extent of its continuity in the face of the gradual increase of iron as a material for making weapons and tools.

The apparent wealth of the population during the Dowris phase, as seen in the abundance of bronze and gold, is also reflected in an agricultural expansion which was taking place at the time. Pollen analyses undertaken at Red Bog in Co. Louth and at Pubble, in Loughermore townland in Co. Derry, suggest that up to about 900–800 bc, there was rough pasture with abundant heaths and brackens, later giving way to blanket peat vegetation. But in the subsequent 300–400 years, down to the middle of the first millennium, there was a phase of intensive agriculture possibly going hand in hand with a further clearance of scrubland, as grasses and plantain show a noticeable increase during that period.

For developments in Ireland during the 700 years or so after 1400 BC we have had to rely largely on a study of the metalwork, with a side glance at the agricultural expansion as glimpsed through the pollen record. The rather lopsided picture which this is liable to give us is the result of our almost total lack of information about most other aspects of the period, which would help us to gain some insight into the social structure of society at the time. It is in many cases only through chance or an excavator coming across Late Bronze Age material when he was expecting something different that we have any knowledge of the few burials and settlements known from this period.

### Elusive burials

The number of burials which can reliably be attributed to the Late Bronze Age can be numbered on the fingers of one hand, largely because gravegoods of metal which might otherwise help us to date the burials were not normally buried with the dead, and because there is, in most instances, no trace above ground which would bring their presence to our notice. One exception was a low cairn of stones in an open area surrounded by a slight circular bank at Carnkenny, Co. Tyrone, where Chris Lynn obtained a radiocarbon date of $c.865$ bc from charcoal found with cremated bone among a total of seventeen pits under the cairn. Further excavation may well show that such cremated burials without gravegoods under round barrows or cairns were the normal burial rite of the period, as Barry Raftery found a somewhat similar pattern recurring within a settlement site which he was excavating at Rathgall, Co. Wicklow. Here, there was a circular ditch enclosing an area some 16 m in diameter, which also contained a number of pits with cremated remains – one representing

85

101

those of an adult, another being those of a child, while a third was a combination of adult and child buried together. Within the enclosure was a U-shaped burned area enclosed by hundreds of closely spaced holes, which may well be the remnants of a funeral pyre. Discarded in the upper part of one of the pits were a small bronze chisel, part of a socketed spearhead and a fragment of a leaf-shaped sword, all of which fit well into the range of material recovered at Dowris.

### Settlements and fortified camps

These Rathgall burials came to light only because they happened to be located within the area of one of the few Late Bronze Age settlements to have been discovered and excavated in Ireland. The site provided considerable traces of settlement, including a number of hearths, and a
102   roughly circular wooden house, 15 m in diameter. This probably belongs to the Late Bronze Age occupation of the site, as a penannular gold ring of around that period was found in a pit in the centre of the house. The house stood in a circular enclosure marked by a bank with a ditch outside it. Much coarse pottery was found, demonstrating the revival of this craft after an apparent lapse of about 700 years. It included bucket-shaped pots with flat rims, rarely decorated but occasionally with perforations beneath the rims for suspension. Also unearthed at Rathgall were saddle querns for grinding wheat, which must therefore have been cultivated at the period. One remarkable find was a beautiful bead or pendant of gold and glass, the latter an unexpected material, which together with simpler glass beads from Rathgall make up the most important group of Late Bronze Age glass objects known from Ireland. But even more important were the 400 fragments of clay moulds for the casting of swords, spearheads and probably socketed axes as well. These were associated with a rectangular timber structure which may be interpreted as the first Late Bronze Age metal workshop to have been recognized in the country.

While it cannot yet be conclusively proved, it is possible that this Late Bronze Age phase of activity at Rathgall may in some way be connected with circular defences around the site, consisting of concentric earthen banks with stone facings. If the defences were even roughly contemporary with the metal workshop, they would provide us not only with one of Ireland's earliest known defences, but also a hillfort dating from the Late Bronze Age. Hillforts have heretofore often been seen as an Iron Age development, but hillforts in the Irish Late Bronze Age would not now be in any way surprising in view of the early first millennium bc dates which have been emerging from British hillforts in recent decades.

Possible evidence for the use of another type of fortification, the promontory fort, at about the same period, came from Dunbeg, Co. Kerry, where T.B. Barry found the earliest phase to consist of a ditch with possible drystone wall and wattle, but as the ditch did not stretch across the whole promontory, it is not certain whether it formed part of a

101,102 **The hillfort of Rathgall, Co. Wicklow** (*Above*) Aerial view of the site under excavation. (*Below*) Remains of a Late Bronze Age house.

fortification, or was just a simple protective barrier. Furthermore, it is only with considerable caution that we should accept the radiocarbon of $c.580$ bc for this earliest phase of occupation on the site, in view of the remarks made above (Chapter 1) about the unreliability of radiocarbon dates falling within the years 800–400 bc.

The use of round houses during the Late Bronze Age may also be attested at Aughinish in Co. Limerick, if we accept Barry Raftery's suggestion for ascribing to this period two oval forts enclosing houses excavated there in advance of the construction of an aluminium plant. If it should transpire that a Late Bronze Age date may also apply to one large and two smaller round houses which happened to come to light at Curraghatoor, Co. Tipperary, during the laying of the Cork-Dublin natural gas pipeline, then we may expect more houses of the kind to be uncovered in the future. But these instances show that the relative paucity of Late Bronze Age houses is not because they did not exist, but rather that they are hard to find because there are no visible traces of them above ground. It is only through chance discovery in the light of such industrial development, or through the fortunate placing of the archaeologist's spade, that we are likely to come across them in the future.

Other than a curious 11.5 m-square timber structure with narrow aisles found at Ballinderry crannog No. 2, in Co. Offaly, and which may have been used for storage or hay-drying, no houses of a domestic nature have come to light among the Late Bronze Age remains excavated on the so-called crannogs, most of which, however, belong to the Christian period. These sites are usually located in shallow water close to the edge of a lake, and usually consist of a small natural shoal piled with stones and brushwood to create a small round or oval island, sometimes linked to the adjacent lake shore by a stone causeway or one of wood which has largely disintegrated. This causeway, the presence of animal bones (cattle, pigs, sheep and goats) and the absence of any convincing Late Bronze Age dwelling-houses, suggest that these man-made islands were not inhabited as fortifications, but served rather as places to enclose a family's flocks and to protect them from animal and human predators. Three human skulls were found beneath floor level at Ballinderry, but it was the bronze socketed knife, fleshhook and flat-rimmed pottery found there which demonstrated that the site was in use during the Late Bronze Age.

Material from the same period was excavated by Joseph Raftery at Knocknalappa, Co. Clare, and at Rathtinaun in Lough Gara on the borders of Sligo and Roscommon, the latter site producing the only hoard of the last millennium BC to have been discovered in an Irish archaeological excavation. In one crannog at Lough Eskragh in Co. Tyrone, Pat Collins found moulds for a leaf-shaped sword, suggesting that a metal workshop had been located there.

But the most remarkable Irish Late Bronze Age settlement of all was that found under the large mound within a circular enclosure at Navan

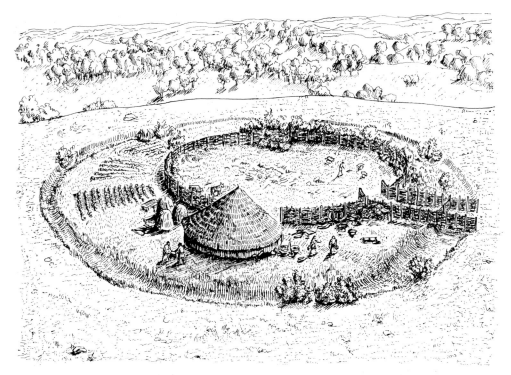

103 Reconstruction of the Late Bronze Age settlement at Navan Fort, Co. Armagh.

Fort in Co. Armagh, which was later to become the great Royal Site of Ulster during the ensuing Iron Age. Here, around 700 BC, a round house was built next to a circular stockade, both of which were enclosed by a circular ditch, as seen in the reconstruction. One of the remarkable features about this site, brilliantly excavated by Dudley Waterman, was that the house was rebuilt nine times and the stockade six times on the same spot in the period from 700–100 BC. Another remarkable feature, which showed this site to be quite exceptional even at the start of its eventful life, was the discovery of the skull of a Barbary ape, which must have come from Spain or North Africa, and which was presumably presented as a special gift to the exalted person who built one of the first houses.

103

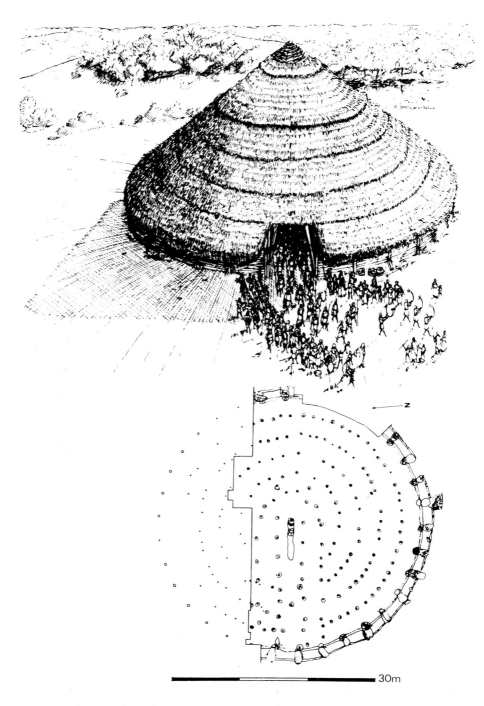

104 Reconstruction of the Iron Age structure at Navan Fort, Co. Armagh.

# 6·The Celtic Iron Age

THE SETTLEMENT LEVELS of the nine successive round houses at Navan Fort in Co. Armagh, which concluded the preceding chapter, produced pottery, lignite bracelets, glass beads, a bronze socketed sickle, a bronze ring-headed pin – and some iron fragments. With this last material, we are introduced to an age when iron began to be adopted gradually as a material for the making of improved weapons and implements. There has been much discussion, though little consensus, about when iron began to become the more standard metal for such purposes. Until the Navan Fort excavation is fully published, it is difficult to assess the role which the advent of iron played in the history of the inhabitants of the site. But in at least one other unpublished site – that at Rathtinaun, Co. Sligo, also mentioned in the previous chapter – iron objects were found in combination with acceptable bronze objects of a normal Late Bronze Age type, including material which can be dated to around the seventh century BC. There would seem to be a possibility that at these two sites we see bronze and iron being worked at around the same time, possibly even as early as the seventh century BC. While these may conceivably be isolated instances, the combination of the two may act as a parallel to the position 2,000 years earlier when copper and gold were worked in a period which was otherwise in many respects a Stone Age. In fact, we have no clear indications that iron was becoming the predominant metal for the making of weapons in Ireland until around the third century BC. But although, from then onwards, we can speak with certainty about the Iron Age in Ireland, bronze continued to be used for the manufacture of jewellery and utilitarian objects such as horse-trappings.

## Royal Sites

We can, with good justification, ascribe to the Iron Age what was undoubtedly the most astonishing monument at Navan Fort, one which 104 was built over the site of the earlier houses. This was a massive circular structure, some 43 m in diameter and probably originally roofed-over. It consisted of a number of concentric rows of upright timbers, those of each ring being spaced about 1.55–2 m apart, and the rings themselves having a space of over 3 m between them. Surrounding these rings on the outside was a further circle of upright timbers, 4 m apart, but this time each was linked to its neighbour by horizontal planking on top, reminiscent of the great trilithons at Stonehenge. From the western perimeter of this outermost circle of timbers, a ramp led downwards to a large hole at the central point of all the concentric timber rings, and in the cavity was a wooden stump of what was clearly once a much taller pole. By measuring the tree-rings, Michael Baillie was able to date the construction of this building to around 100 BC.

But even more extraordinary than this wooden structure was the fact that, at some stage probably not long after its completion, it was covered over by a limestone cairn of stones with an outer envelope of turf and topsoil, the whole mound measuring about 50 m in diameter, and reaching a height of about 5–6 m. Dudley Waterman was able to reconstruct the original wooden structure because its decayed timbers were left as voids in the body of the mound, but he also discovered that a deliberate fire had destroyed the outermost timber structure with the planks adjoining it. Such an extraordinary structure is unlikely to have been used for ordinary domestic purposes, and the fact that the timber parts were purposely covered over by the stone mound can only lead to the presumption that the whole must have been created for some ritual purpose. The ritual nature of the site is further underlined by the fact that this structure, and the houses which preceded it, were encircled by a bank with a ditch *inside*, not outside it, which is what we would have expected had the bank been constructed for defensive purposes. It must be said, though, that the date of the bank and ditch, and their correlation with a particular stage in the construction of the buildings, has yet to be established. It is interesting, certainly, that the ditch inside the bank is a feature found in Early Bronze Age henges in southern England, and the

105 Aerial view of Navan Fort, Co. Armagh, before excavation.

comparison between the outermost wooden uprights linked at the top by horizontal timbers at Navan Fort on the one hand, and the trilithons of Stonehenge on the other, leads to speculation that the Navan Fort monument may be an Iron Age reincarnation of a much earlier henge monument, which may – like Navan Fort itself – have served as a ritual centre for the surrounding community.

Navan Fort is generally equated with Emhain Macha (pron., Ow-en Mock-a), the royal seat of the Ulaid, whose most famous king was Connor. He was protected from invaders from the south by the great Irish hero Cú Chulainn (pron., Coo Hullin) in the series of early Irish tales known as the Ulster cycle, of which the most famous is the *Táin Bó Cuailgne* (pron., Thaw-in Bow Koo-il-nge), *The Cattle Raid of Cooley*. Perhaps the houses which Dudley Waterman excavated at Navan Fort represent the early phases of the Ulaid rise to power, and the timber structure and mound its visual confirmation. It is certainly the most important royal site in the early history of Ulster. 105

But it was not the only one in Ireland. Another was Dún Ailinne, otherwise Knockaulin, near Kilcullen in Co. Kildare, which would appear to have been the most important of the royal sites in south Leinster. Like Navan Fort, too, its equally undated ditch is placed inside the bank which encloses 13.8 hectares (34 acres) of this prominent hill-top site. Excavations carried out there by Bernard Wailes in the late 1960s and early 1970s showed an earlier Neolithic occupation of the site – a feature which Dudley Waterman had also encountered at Navan Fort. The first 106

106 Aerial view of Dún Ailinne, Co. Kildare, during excavation.

traces of presumed Iron Age habitation consisted of a circular palisade trench, 22 m in diameter, which originally held upright wooden posts. A road, probably also Iron Age in date, seems to have led up to whatever structure the palisade may have contained. Subsequently, perhaps around 250 bc or even later, three concentric rings of timber uprights were erected closely together, of which the outermost was deemed to have been the highest. Bernard Wailes interpreted these rings as either two parapet walks, or as two tiers of seats for spectators partaking in some function in the central area which the rings enclosed. This central area, which had a diameter of 28.5 m, he took to be unroofed. A few hundred years later, two further concentric palisades surrounding a circle of large upright timber posts was built on almost exactly the same spot and – reminiscent of the happenings at Navan Fort – they were later burned and subsequently removed before a small mound was built over them.

### Ritual stones

As Dún Ailinne shows little trace of having been inhabited in any permanent fashion, we can only conclude that it may have been a site used for some occasional or even seasonal ritual, of which we have no knowledge. Ritual, too, or what can surely only be taken as ritual, is the probable role of a very different type of monument – the decorated stone. By far the best known of these is the Turoe Stone, near Bullaun in Co. Galway, dating from the last few centuries BC. It is a granite boulder 1.68 m high, which was moved to its present position from somewhere close to a ringfort known as the Rath of Feerwore. It has been dressed into the shape of a domed cylinder, having a step-like pattern incised horizontally around its middle. The upper 78 cm is covered with three-plane, curvilinear ornament, cleverly assembled from an anthology of basic motifs such as 'trumpet-ends', triskeles, and even stylized animal heads, some of the designs being present in both positive and negative forms. It was Michael Duignan who unravelled from these complex designs the fact that the ornament is in four parts, two triangular and two conjoined shield shapes placed opposite one another, suggesting that the lay-out – which may have had the separate elements originally picked out in a variety of colours long since vanished – was derived from a four-faced stone or wooden pillar, of which one stone example survives in Brittany. But there is now fairly general agreement that the patterns on the Turoe Stone – which must ultimately stem from the third-century BC art style of the continental Celts – is best paralleled on Celtic objects of Britain and Ireland, rather than on those from Brittany. What purpose the stone originally fulfilled, and indeed what the idea behind the quadrupartite design was, remains unknown, and it is idle to speculate on whether the four faces could have been intended to represent the four corners of the earth, or whether the stone – like the omphalos stone at Delphi – may even have been a centre for oracular divinations.

107

108

107,108 **The Turoe Stone, Co. Galway** (*Right*) General view. (*Below*) Roll-out drawing of the La-Tène-style decoration.

109 The Iron Age decorated stone at Castlestrange, Co. Roscommon.

It is likely that there may have been a number of such monuments carved in wood in Iron Age Ireland, and the swelling lobes carved on wooden pieces of the early Islamic Samarra style show just how well the motifs of the Turoe Stone could have looked if carved in wood. But there are a few other surviving Irish stones which have, or may have had, a domed upper part like that of the Turoe Stone, though their designs differ from it, and they are not as competently laid out or carved. One of these is 109 at Castlestrange in the neighbouring county of Roscommon. A further example, possibly quadrupartite in design, and which is now in the National Museum in Dublin, came from Killycluggin in Co. Cavan, though excavations undertaken at the site failed to shed any light on possible ritual surroundings for the stone.

## Swords and scabbards

The decoration on these stones has a certain affinity with that found on a
number of sword-scabbards or sheaths found particularly in Co. Antrim. 110, 111
The Irish Iron Age swords themselves number less than two dozen, and
are much shorter than similar Iron Age weapons associated with Celtic
cultures elsewhere in Europe, thus suggesting that they are of native
manufacture. But the lack of decoration on the iron swords is in stark
contrast with the scabbards from Co. Antrim which may be taken as being
among the earliest examples in Ireland of a type of decoration described as
La Tène, named after a site in Switzerland where this typically Celtic
ornament was first identified as such in the middle of the last century. The
style had developed in Central Europe in the fifth century BC, drawing
heavily on Greek/Etruscan motifs, with an admixture of Oriental, even
Scythian elements. Towards the end of the fourth century BC, under
strong influence from Italy, a new variant known as the Waldalgesheim
style emerged in the Rhine area – and it is echoes of this particular version
that we find on the Irish scabbards, best exemplified on those found in the
last century at Lisnacroghera, Co. Antrim. Doubt has been cast on the 110
report of the discovery which describes the find-spot as a crannog, as it
might also have been a centre for some kind of votive deposit.

Other scabbards have come from the river Bann, also in Co. Antrim. 111
These scabbards have engraved decoration, of variable but often high
quality, which is spread over the whole surface of the scabbard, and while
they would all appear to be the products of one 'culture' – if not indeed of a
single workshop – they do show a refreshing variety in their ornament.
The designs tend to be symmetrical, sometimes – as on the scabbard
known as Lisnacroghera, No. 2 – divided by a central line down the
middle, with mirror-image decoration forming lyre-shaped patterns. The
motifs include S-figures like running waves, tightly coiled spirals and
stylized plant ornament. This last feature shows its derivation from the
same Waldalgesheim style which influenced the design of the Turoe
Stone, and which is also found on scabbards from France and Hungary
around the third century BC. The ultimate inspiration for the decoration
on the Ulster scabbards must have come from the Continent, even from as
far away as Hungary. Martin Jope and Barry Raftery have both pleaded
for direct continental influence for the Irish scabbards, rather than seeing
England as having acted as an intermediate filter, as other scholars have
argued. The date of the Irish scabbards is difficult to ascertain precisely,
but they would seem to fit best into the period around the third or even the
second century BC.

Spears were obviously used frequently by Iron Age warriors in
Ireland. This is most evident from the number of bronze spearbutts (for
the feet of the spears, as it were), of which sixty-five are known. They are,
with few exceptions, peculiar to Ireland, and some are decorated in the La
Tène style. One group of spearbutts resembles a door-knob, which would

110,111 **Decorated bronze scabbards** (*Left*) Scabbards from Lisnacroghera, Co. Antrim. (*Opposite*) Detail of the decoration on a bronze scabbard from the river Bann at Toome, Co. Antrim.

5 cm

5 cm

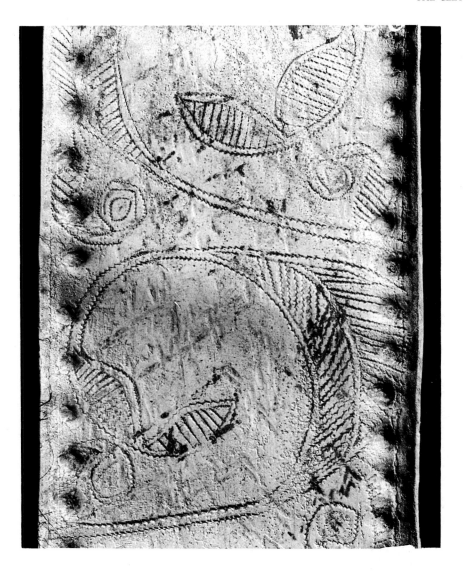

seem to be a most impractical shape to speed a spear upon its flight-path, but Lisnacroghera has provided evidence that they were, in fact, attached to the end of a spear, though some of them may of course have been used more for ceremonial purposes. In curious contrast, the number of spearheads which can be ascribed to the Iron Age is very much smaller, because of the few characteristic features which allow attribution of individual specimens to this period. However, some – such as those from Boho, Co. Fermanagh or Corofin, Co. Clare – bear ornament which, by analogy, may help us to date the spears to the Iron Age. Also in contrast to the spearbutts, the spearheads are of iron, not of bronze.

112 Detail of the decoration on a bronze snaffle-bit found at Attymon, Co. Galway.

113 Block-wheel from Doogarymore, Co. Roscommon.

The most numerous of all pieces of La Tène bronze metalwork to survive in Ireland are those associated with horses – horse-bits and strange Y-shaped pieces of uncertain use. The horse-bits are most often made of five separate pieces, including rings for the reins attached at either end. What are taken to be the earlier bits have little ornament, but later examples – such as those from Attymon, Co. Galway – have attractive La Tène 112 decoration on the two main pieces of the bit. The considerable numbers of both the Y-shaped pieces and the horse-bits themselves give us a picture of a society in which the horse played an important role. Some of the horse-bits show wear particularly on one side, which may have resulted from their having been used by horses pulling a two-horse chariot. But objects which can be identified as having formed part of such chariots are few in number, and even the position on the chariot of those which do survive is uncertain. The only wheels which survive complete from the Iron Age are the large solid wooden three-piece wheels from Doogarymore, Co. Roscommon, which gave radiocarbon dates of *c*.450 and *c*.365 bc respectively. By no 113 stretch of the imagination could they be considered as having belonged to a speedy chariot. Instead, they should be seen as having been used on a heavy agricultural vehicle of the kind one can still see today being drawn by two oxen on the Anatolian plateau.

It is a cart rather than a chariot that we would expect to have been driven along the wooden trackway which Barry Raftery excavated at 115 Corlea, Co. Longford, as he found parts of what seems to be a cart beside it. This road, almost $\frac{5}{8}$ mile (1 km) long, consisted of two parallel runners on which oak sleepers were placed close together at right angles. On the basis of the tree-rings, Michael Baillie was able to establish that the trees were felled in the spring of the year 148 BC. An older, but smaller pedestrian trackway was also discovered close by, but its date has not yet been established. Such trackways must have become increasingly necessary with the gradual expansion of bog growth at this period.

From descriptions in old Irish literature, David Greene reconstructed 114 the old Irish chariot of the heroic tales as 'a simple two-wheeled cart, containing two single seats in tandem in a light wooden frame, and drawn by horses harnessed by bridles to a yoke attached to the chariot pole; the wheels were shod with iron tyres'. He pointed out also that there may have been two shafts protruding from the back of the vehicle, which makes it sound suspiciously like the forerunner of the cart still drawn by a single horse or donkey in certain parts of Ireland today. The evidence for this reconstruction comes, among others, from the Ulster cycle – that series of tales extolling the feats of the great hero Cú Chulainn. These tales were not written down before the seventh century AD, but Kenneth Jackson has suggested that – like Homer's *Iliad* – they present us with 'a window on the Iron Age', mirroring a bygone heroic society which existed in the prehistoric period before St Patrick's time. This was a society in which the blacksmith, maker of weapons, was someone held in high esteem, a world in which druids played a part as prophets and soothsayers, and where an aristocracy of champions, eager for fame, spent their time fighting one another in single combat. These heroes had round shields and spears, but the sword seems to have been of lesser importance, though one was wielded by Cú Chulainn himself. The young warrior, on reaching manhood, was given a spear and a shield, and an important part of his initiation rite was the ceremonial mounting of a chariot. He would then proceed to battle, and would cut off the heads of his defeated opponents and bring them home as a trophy, and at the celebratory feast afterwards he would try to claim the champion's portion in the presence of his fellow-warriors in some great banqueting hall.

Such is the picture painted for us in the old Irish heroic tales. But an astonishingly similar state of affairs among the real-life Celts of Gaul around or shortly after 100 BC has been transmitted to us through quotations from Posidonius, or summaries of his work in classical Greek and Latin authors such as Athenaeus, Diodorus Siculus, Strabo and even Julius Caesar himself. Here we find the bards, the soothsayers and the druid philosophers, the decapitated heads of the enemy serving as a trophy, and the champion's portion being claimed at the feast. Are we to interpret the similarity between the continental Celts as described by

114,115 **Chariots and tracks** (*Above*) Reconstruction of an old Irish 'chariot'. (*Below*) Trackway tree-ring dated to 148 BC, found in a bog at Corlea, Co. Longford, with what seems to be parts of a cart beside it.

classical authors, and the Irish situation as found in the Ulster cycle, as merely a reflection of a common Celtic model for both societies, or ought we to imagine the continental Celts as having come to Ireland – directly or through Britain – in the last few centuries BC, as the continental background of the Lisnacroghera and river Bann sword-scabbards could suggest? Was it they who made the country so totally Celtic in its language, laws and institutions, that there was scarcely a trace of any non-Celtic elements in Ireland by the time St Patrick arrived?

110, 111

### When did the Celts come to Ireland?

This brings us to the vexed and still unsolved question as to when the Celts arrived in Ireland or, put another way, when was a language ancestral to modern Gaelic first spoken in Ireland? As there seems to be no other Indo-European language other than Celtic which came to Ireland, the question can be rephrased as: when did the speakers of an Indo-European language first reach Ireland? Obviously they must have come in sufficient numbers to make the country entirely Celtic-speaking by the dawn of the historic period in the early years of Christianity in Ireland. People have, therefore, in the past sought evidence in the archaeological record for invasions on a sufficiently massive scale to have brought about this celticization. There is, frankly, no certainty to be gained in the matter from the archaeological evidence. There are a number of possibilities, yet when considering them we should keep in mind the effects of two historically known invasions, those of the Vikings – who had little effect on the language of the country, and the Normans – who for centuries managed to convert only certain parts of the country to the use of their language.

What, firstly, of an invasion by the continental La Tène Celts, who dominated half of Europe before the rise of Rome? Such a notion could find support in the decoration of the Irish sword-scabbards having been derived possibly from Gaul, and ultimately from the middle Danube, during the third or second century BC. In addition, some of the behavioural traits of the continental Celts of around 100 BC, as noted by Posidonius, recur in a remarkably similar form in the heroic society described in the tales of the Ulster cycle, first written down more than half a millennium later. As an example, one may quote the comparison between the use of chariots in Gaulish warfare and the way in which the Ulster hero Cú Chulainn is said to have gone into battle mounted on his chariot. But, contrasting with such arguments, is the fact that chariot burials and their accompanying gravegoods, as found on the Continent particularly in the fifth and fourth centuries BC, and occasionally later, are hitherto unknown in Ireland. Furthermore, because the decoration and nature of the La Tène-ornamented bronze pieces from Ireland, apart from the sword-scabbards, are sufficiently different from those in England, and – as in the case of the spearbutts and Y-shaped pieces –

116 A gold torc found at Clonmacnois, Co. Offaly. It had been imported into Ireland, perhaps from eastern Gaul or the Middle Rhine.

almost entirely peculiar to Ireland, they would argue against any large-scale La Tène invasion either from the Continent or Britain. Any direct imports of the period, such as a small bronze figure from Etruria, or the superb gold torc or neck-ring from the middle Rhine area found at Clonmacnois, Co. Offaly, could easily have come to Ireland by way of normal trade or barter. The introduction of the La Tène art style could have come about by the arrival of only a few craftsmen, and even if they did come as part of a warrior's retinue, is the evidence strong enough for an all-pervading celticization in language and customs by them?

Another factor to be borne in mind is that the distribution of La Tène material in Ireland is concentrated in the northern half of the country. Seamus Caulfield has recently suggested that the beehive quern (a variety of rotary quern shaped like an old-fashioned beehive), which is an Iron Age introduction largely confined to the northern half of Ireland, is indicative of a group of La Tène immigrants from southern Scotland or northern England. But do we have here – like the modern washing machine – the adoption of an energy-saving device by an already settled population, rather than evidence for the arrival of a new group of people bringing their grinding expertise with them?

What, then, of the celticization of the southern half of the country? Etienne Rynne suggested that 'La Tène' reached Ireland along two routes – an earlier one, directly from France into the west of Ireland, exemplified by the Turoe Stone, and a later one from Britain into the northern half of Ireland, as mirrored in the decorated sword-scabbards. But if the decoration of the Turoe Stone is now seen as being derived essentially from Britain, then the case for the celticization of the south and west of

Ireland directly from France is weakened. Caulfield sees the celticization of the non-La Tène southern half of Ireland as possible, if the Celts were to be considered as having come to Ireland from Spain. One support for this was seen in the tale told in the medieval scholastic *Book of Invasions* (Chapter 1), whereby Míl or Milesius, the ancestor of the Gaels of Ireland, came from Spain, landing in the south of Ireland according to one version of the tale. But the name Míl is seen by many as being derived from *Miles hispaniae*, a Roman Spanish soldier, and thus scarcely Celtic at all, and *The Book of Invasions* has been considered by most authorities as little more than a figment of scholastic imagination.

People who may have spoken a Q-Celtic language, which Gaelic is, could have come from Spain in the wake of the Roman conquest there in 133 BC. Such a possibility is strengthened by the presence of *chevaux-de-frise*, stones placed closely together for defensive purposes outside the walls of stone forts at, among other places, Dún Aenghus on the Aran Islands in Co. Galway, for similar examples occur in Spain and northern Portugal. *Chevaux-de-frise*, however, have been discovered in wooden form in Germany and Belgium, where they are earlier than the Spanish or Irish examples. It is possibly not without significance in this context that the Fír Bolg, one of the mythical peoples who – again according to the *Book of Invasions* – entered Ireland before Míl and who, in medieval legend, are the builders of Dún Aenghus and other stone forts on the Aran Islands, are associated by some philologists with the Belgae whom Caesar conquered in France and Belgium. But if the descendants of the Belgae were responsible for building Dún Aenghus, the *chevaux-de-frise* there are more likely to have come from Belgium to Ireland via Britain, rather than directly from Spain. Even if we were to expect an Iron Age influx from Spain, would it have been of sufficient dimensions to have made the south, if not indeed the whole, of Ireland so totally Celtic? The evidence is not strong enough for us to think so.

The *Ora Maritima*, written by Avienus in the middle of the fourth century AD, is recognized as containing elements of an early Greek exploratory voyage dating, from internal evidence, to around the sixth century BC, and it contains references to Celtic tribes on the North Sea as well as in France and Spain at the time. This puts the existence of Celtic tribes on the Continent back into the Hallstatt period, which preceded the La Tène culture. Could peoples of the Hallstatt culture have brought the Celtic language to Ireland, if evidence from the La Tène period is not cumulatively strong enough? The main evidence which could be adduced in favour of this theory is the finding of a number of swords of Hallstatt type in Ireland. But these Hallstatt swords would not appear – in the absence of a whole range of accompanying material or burial rites – to provide sufficient evidence for a large scale 'invasion' either, although they seem to be local imitations of swords developed in England or on the Continent. The same argument could also be taken to apply to the Late

134

Bronze Age swords which, however, could be seen as the successors of Bronze Age rapiers, thus suggesting continuity rather than innovation in warring techniques.

Of the few Iron Age burials known in Ireland, be it cremation in ring-barrows or inhumation burials, none can clearly be shown to be earlier than the first millennium AD. If anything, they would argue in favour of the continuation of earlier indigenous burial types, and they contain no gravegoods of clearly foreign origin, with the possible exception of glass beads, and the contents of a burial of the second century AD to be discussed below. In short, surviving archaeological material gives no absolutely reliable indication of any large-scale Celtic invasion of the country during the Iron Age or the Later Bronze Age. Nevertheless, philologists like David Greene see in the Iron Age period after 500 BC the introduction of the Celtic language which is ancestral to that still spoken in Ireland today.

As Indo-European languages are unlikely to have reached Central Europe much earlier than 3000 bc, it seems scarcely possible that the first builders of megalithic tombs, let alone the country's first farmers or even earliest inhabitants, were speakers of an Indo-European tongue. Another possibility which has been considered for the introduction of an Indo-European language is the period at the transition from the Late Neolithic to the Early Bronze Age, which saw the introduction of Beaker pottery and the development of the Food Vessel, the increasing popularity of metal, and the widespread establishment of the single burial, contrasting with the communal burial practice of the megaliths. If, as much of current opinion holds, Beakers only represent a 'package' rather than a new people, then, with Ireland already having a tradition of Stone Age single burials, the case for seeing the first Celtic speakers arriving at the beginning of the Bronze Age is weakened. However, although the rise of the Food Vessel pottery must nevertheless be considered as representing a possible arrival of new people whose short skulls contrast with the longer skulls known from Neolithic burials, evidence for a large-scale invasion in Ireland at the beginning of the Bronze Age is still as unproven as it is for the earlier periods. In contrast to half a century ago, when archaeologists saw every major new development as the sign of an 'invasion', recent trends tend now to play these down as explanations for cultural change.

If the search for large-scale 'invasions' in the Irish archaeological record proves negative, it is perhaps more advisable to see the arrival of Indo-European or Celtic-speaking peoples as a gradual process which took place not at one fell swoop causing great upheavals in society, but peacefully over hundreds if not thousands of years – Hawkes's concept of 'cumulative Celticity'. The process may well have begun during the Early Bronze Age, but an effort by James Mallory to achieve even the smallest degree of consensus among Irish archaeologists and linguists on the matter led only to the premise that the arrival of the Celts in Ireland was

52
61, 62

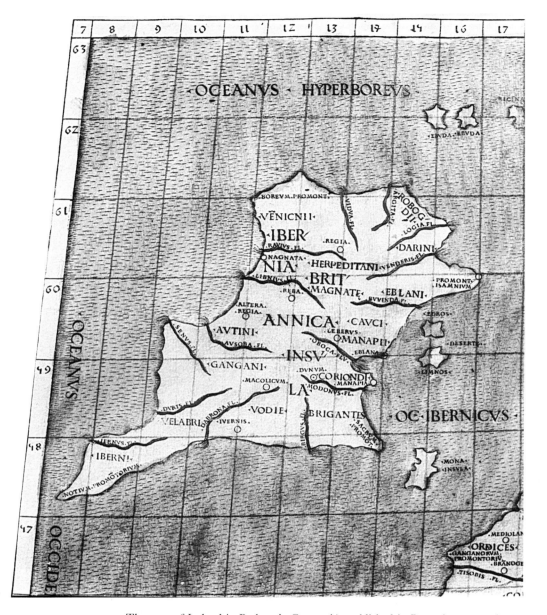

117 The map of Ireland in Ptolemy's *Geographia* published in Rome in 1490 – the first edition to include the location of tribes, rivers and places.

less likely to have taken place in the second rather than in the first millennium BC. With this uncertainty we should possibly see the similarities between the Ulster cycle of tales and the Celtic society as described by Posidonius around 100 BC as containing a considerable number of traits inherited from some earlier common ancestors.

## Greeks and Romans

Another Greek source which throws further interesting light on Iron Age
Ireland is Ptolemy's map, a gazetteer allegedly giving information on a    117
total of fifty-five rivers, tribes, towns and islands in Ireland around the
second century AD. But the light becomes more opaque when we imagine
the number of different tongues and mouths the original material must
have gone through before ending up as the Greek names which Ptolemy
gives. There is no 'original' version of Ptolemy's map, and the grid lay-out
which he provided is the basis for the modern locations of his names – the
oldest surviving version of the map, dating from AD 1490, having gone
through the further stage of having Ptolemy's Greek names transliterated
into Latin. A number of the names sound distinctly non-Irish and suggest
the presence of British traders as the potential source for at least some of
Ptolemy's information. It is not impossible, indeed, that there were
British settlements in Ireland during the early centuries AD, that is,
during the period of Roman occupation in Britain.

There is no reliable evidence that the Roman army ever set foot in
Ireland – scarcely because they were afraid of the Irish, but rather because
they felt that an invasion would probably contribute little if anything to
the coffers of Rome. Ireland, not being a part of the Roman Empire, had
its traditional direct maritime links with the Continent severed after the
Roman conquest of Gaul, but Ptolemy's informants are at least sufficient
evidence for trade contacts between Britain and Ireland in the second
century AD, and possibly even half a century earlier when Ptolemy's
source, Philemon, would seem to have been gathering his information.
Even though Ireland became more isolated after the Roman invasion of
Britain, there are nevertheless slight indications of trade going in both
directions, and the development of the La Tène art style on Irish bronze
objects of the century on either side of 1 AD may also point to some
inspiration from Britain.

After the propitious start to the La Tène decoration in Ireland on the
Ulster scabbards in the third to second centuries BC, a new development
made itself felt in the succeeding two centuries with the introduction of
the use of compass-made arcs in the design of motifs. This latter is clearly
seen on the incised decoration of a series of bone plaques which may have
been part of a temporary workshop located in one of the passage-tombs at
Loughcrew, Co. Meath. In bronze, the new style makes an attractive
appearance on the mounts from Somerset, Co. Galway, and Cornalaragh,    118
Co. Monaghan, with their intriguing *trompe l'oeil* and positive/negative
designs. The hoard from Somerset, dating from around the early part of
the first century AD, is important, firstly, because it includes a number of
individual pieces which help to connect it with certain well-known Irish
objects which were found in isolation. The duck-headed handle of a bowl
from Somerset, for instance, is close to that of a fine turned-bronze bowl
from Keshcarrigan, Co. Leitrim, which has sometimes been considered to    119

have been an import from England; the Somerset find, however, makes it likely to be a show-piece for the high quality of Irish bronze craftsmanship around the turn of the millennium. The hoard also contains a fibula, or brooch, like the one from Navan Fort in Co. Armagh, which seems to be an Irish adaptation of an English mirror-handle to a brooch-type of Celtic ancestry. A number of earlier Irish brooches had been modelled on Celtic fibulae on the Continent. But the Somerset hoard is important, secondly, because the mount with the compass-designed *trompe l'oeil* motif introduces us to a whole range of objects of the first century BC/first century AD, which show the Irish craftsmen giving new life to their compass designs by the addition of plastic forms in relief.

120

121

118

118–121 **Art of the Irish Celts**
(*Opposite*) Eye-deceiving
decoration on the lid of a bronze
box found at Somerset,
Co. Galway. (*Left*) A bird-head
was clearly the model for the
handle on a bronze bowl from
Keshcarrigan, Co. Leitrim.
(*Above*) An Iron Age brooch
from Navan Fort, Co. Armagh.
(*Below*) Iron Age fibulae from,
left to right: Clogher,
Co. Tyrone; Dún Aenghus,
Aran Islands, Co. Galway; and
without provenance.

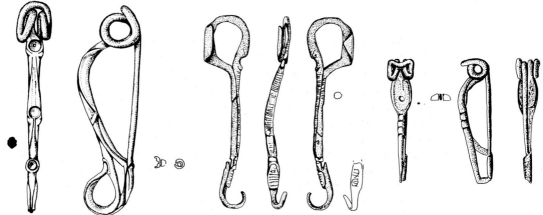

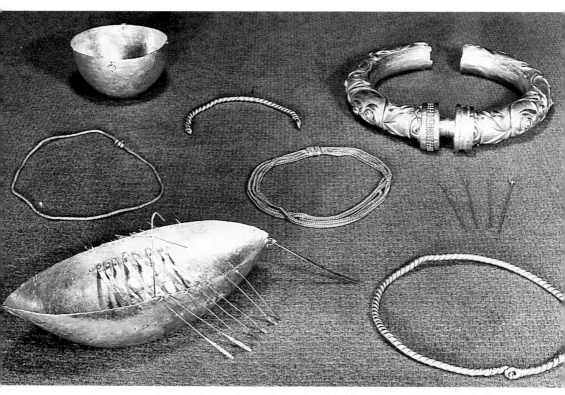

122,123 **The Broighter hoard** (*Above*) Gold objects from the hoard, including a model boat and torc or neck-ring. (*Opposite*) Drawing of the torc and a detail of its remarkable decoration.

122    One of the most dramatic examples is found on a beautiful gold torc or neck-band of around the last half-century BC found at Broighter in Co. Derry, which heightens the motifs by the provision of spirals rising from

123    the surface like a snail's shell. The ornament resembles that on a find from Snettisham in Norfolk, England, and its buffer terminals and T-shaped joining piece are so like other terminals on continental torcs that some have considered the Broighter torc – or at least its terminals – to have been imported from the Continent. But while no foreign parallels can be seen to combine all the features on the torc, it is interesting that it was found (in circumstances which gave rise to a famous law case in 1903) together with

122    other gold objects, including a remarkable model boat with fifteen oars, nine seats and a mast with a yard arm, the first evidence for the use of sail in Irish waters. In 56 BC, Caesar defeated the Celtic Veneti, a seafaring tribe in Brittany, by cutting down their sails, and one may be forgiven for speculating that the Broighter boat might have been made by one of the Veneti who perhaps fled to Ireland from Caesar's wrath, thus helping to explain the presence of the sail.

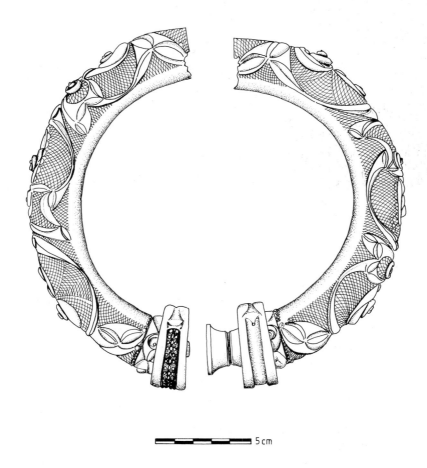

124 A human head decorates the handle of a dagger from Ballyshannon, Co. Donegal.

124 And could those wire necklaces of Mediterranean origin, which also formed a part of the Broighter hoard, have possibly reached Ireland via Brittany too? Perhaps the continental dagger handle from Ballyshannon, Co. Donegal, could also have come to Ireland on the same wave, and it is even possible that Venetic refugees may have fortified themselves in some of the Irish coastal promontory forts of the kind frequently found in their Breton homeland, even though there is no evidence to support such a theory. A further maritime connection may be seen in Richard Warner's suggestion that the boat and torc, as well as other gold objects apparently deposited with them, were dedicated to the Celtic sea god, Manannán Mac Lir.

125 Disc decorated in the La Tène style, found in the river Bann.

Possibly slightly later, and belonging to around the first century AD, are three objects related in design and technique, which form the high point in Irish La Tène art. These are a disc from Loughan Island in the river Bann, Co. Derry, the unprovenanced 'Petrie Crown', named after the collector/archaeologist who owned it in the last century, and the horns found in Cork in 1909. All of these items, of uncertain use, are decorated with elegant and infinitely subtle compass-drawn trumpet and lentoid curves, and two of them have stylized bird-heads among their ornament. What makes these objects so special is not only their superlative rhythmic patterns, but also the way in which the designs were made to stand out from the curved surfaces by the cutting away of the background surface,

125
126
127

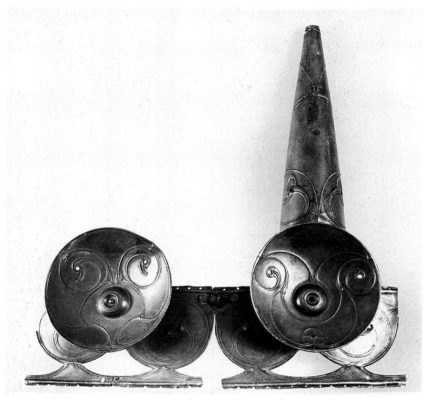

126 The so-called 'Petrie Crown', part of what may have been a bronze crown, named after the antiquary George Petrie, in whose collection it first appeared. Ht 15 cm.

as Michael J. O'Kelly showed in his masterly technical survey of these objects. Related in style, though perhaps later in date, are a group of
128 dished objects known as Monasterevan discs, after the findspot of two of them, where the relief decoration – made to resemble the shape of a stylized human face – has however been achieved by the ornament being hammered up from the back.

This group of objects, dating from around the first century AD, though uniquely Irish in their form, and spread over wide areas of the country in their distribution, show in such features as the stylized bird-heads a certain connection with the Celtic decorated objects from various parts of western Britain. It is of interest in this context, too, that a small number of objects identified by Barry Raftery as Irish have been found in Britain, in the same way that a number of actual imports from Roman Britain have been recognized in Ireland.

The Roman material in Ireland falls into two clear chronological groupings. The first can be ascribed to the first or second centuries AD, and the second to the fourth and early fifth centuries. Among the first
129 group can be numbered some burials. Those found on Lambay Island,

127 The enigmatic horns discovered in Cork in 1909.

Co. Dublin, include one grave which probably contained a shield-boss and sword, as well as decorated sheet-bronze plaques and a mirror, while others contained brooches. Etienne Rynne has argued convincingly that the graves may well have been the burials of a small group of Celtic Brigantians from the north of England, who had been in contact with Roman cultures further south in England, but who had fled to the Irish coast (perhaps from Wales) in the face of the Roman thrust into northern Britain in AD 71. The sherd of Roman pottery alleged to have been found

128 Bronze disc, cast and decorated by hammering, with a stylized representation of the human face. Found at Monasterevan, Co. Kildare. Diameter *c*. 30 cm.

on the large promontory fort at Loughshinny, on the mainland opposite Lambay Island, may also have been associated with the same refugees. More unexpected, because it is so far inland, is the discovery in the last century of a cremation burial of the second century AD at Stonyford, Co. Kilkenny, which contained two Roman glass vessels and a Roman mirror. 130 Richard Warner has suggested that this find might imply the presence of a Roman trading station in the vicinity. He has also postulated that some Roman material in Ireland could have come through Irish people serving as mercenaries in Britain – a possible explanation for the leather shield, resembling a Roman type, found at Clonoura, Co. Tipperary, which 131 however is more likely to be Irish than Roman.

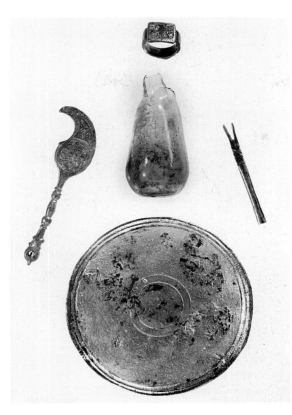

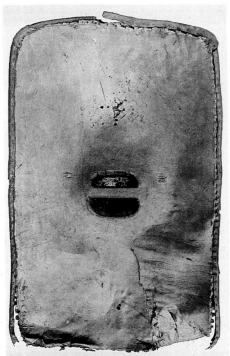

129–131 **Roman contacts** (*Opposite*) One of a number of Roman brooches discovered at Lambay, Co. Dublin. (*Above*) A glass bottle, bronze disc and other objects of Roman origin said to have come from a grave at Stonyford, Co. Kilkenny. (*Right*) A leather shield, resembling a Roman type, from Clonoura, Co. Tipperary.

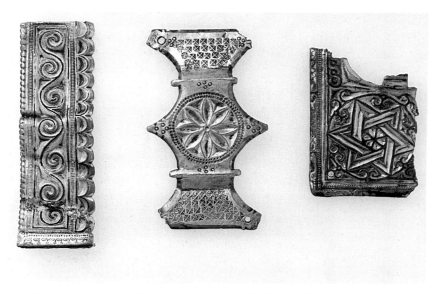

132 Roman decorated metalwork from a hoard at Ballinrees, Co. Derry.

132    The second group of Roman material in Ireland dates from the fourth or early fifth centuries AD, after an almost complete gap in the third century. This later group includes coins, and some gold objects found outside Newgrange, which even then must have retained its aura of mystery and sanctity, or have been at the time – as it still is today – a tourist attraction. The later grouping also contains hoards of Roman silver in various stages of repair or disrepair from Ballinrees near Coleraine, Co. Derry, and Balline, Co. Limerick. The considerable number of coins, some of them in hoards, may be explained by the Irish making raids on a decaying Late Roman Empire, and taking with them as booty human slaves, one of whom was the young St Patrick.

   It was probably also during the period of this later grouping of Roman material that Irish tribes from Munster – the Dési and the Uí Liatháin – settled in parts of western Britain, particularly in north and south Wales and even as far south as Cornwall, perhaps to give some support to the Britons in driving out the Romans from British soil. It was not until the fifth century at the earliest that these Irish in Wales erected stones with Ogham inscriptions, the letters being indicated by notches crossing or on either side of a central line – usually the corner of a stone. Many Ogham stones are also found in Ireland, and particularly in Munster, but whether the Irish who went to Wales brought the knowledge of Ogham with them, or whether they could have helped to adapt it from the Roman alphabet into a 'secret language', and bring it back with them to Ireland in the fifth century, we cannot say. These Ogham stones, usually with a commemorative inscription naming a person and a progenitor or ancestor, are the first surviving traces of Irish writing, and they almost certainly continued in use for a variety of purposes well into the Christian period. At about the same time as the Munster men were colonizing Wales, the Dál Riada, an Antrim tribe, were also establishing a colony across the North Channel in Scotland. They were indeed the Scots (originally a name for the Irish) who later gave their name to the whole country which they subsequently conquered from the Picts. But that is a story which brings us beyond the time span of the present volume, although smaller Irish settlements may have been made in southwestern Scotland in the centuries before Christianity came to Ireland.

## Hillforts

Roman material, including a coin of Constantine, of $c.337-340$, was found in the habitation levels of the hillfort at Freestone Hill, Co. Kilkenny, excavated by Gerhard Bersu. The fort itself, consisting of a stone wall with a ditch outside it, covers an area of about 2 hectares (5 acres). We have seen already in the last chapter how Rathgall showed evidence of Late Bronze Age habitation within the surrounding earthen bank, though the relationship between the Bronze Age material and the construction of the defences could not be proven. Evidence from Britain, however, is making a case for the Late Bronze Age beginnings of hillfort building ever more likely. Yet although, in Britain, a considerable amount of pre-Roman Iron Age material has come to light in hillforts, and the same is true of the large *oppida* on the Continent, very little material of this period has yet been uncovered on the corresponding Irish sites. A brooch, possibly of the first century AD, as well as pottery, a pin and a brooch of the first or second century AD, have been found in Richard Warner's excavations at Clogher in Co. Tyrone. These, and a second-century Roman military strap-tag found at Rathgall, testify to some degree of habitation between the Late Bronze Age occupation levels and the late Roman material exemplified from Freestone Hill.

These excavated examples, however, are but a very small sample of the fifty or so hillforts known throughout the country, and future research at other sites may well provide more evidence for a fuller Iron Age occupation of Irish hillforts. Barry Raftery has shown that, by and large, hillforts in Ireland may be divided into three different categories. The first of these, including Freestone Hill, has just a single line of defence and, in a number of cases, the line of fortification encloses a hill-top on which there are traces of earlier burials – be it a passage-tomb, as in the case of Baltinglass Hill in Co. Wicklow for instance, or an Early Bronze Age cairn, as at Freestone Hill. This has naturally given rise to speculation as to whether the Late Bronze Age or Iron Age inhabitants purposely chose a defensible hill-top location which had already been 'sanctified' by the presence of a burial site of earlier generations, thus suggesting a certain continuity of local populations over a millennium or more, during which the ancestral burial places would have continued to be hallowed. Alternatively, the choice of site could be construed as new population elements grafting themselves onto the older, more established, traditions, in order to become respectable and to establish a greater ancestry for their particular dynasty. But the Freestone Hill population, even if only temporary, showed scant respect for the Early Bronze Age burials on the site: they carried away most of the cairn stones for the construction of a defensive wall. Most of the hillforts of the first, single-defence category, tend to be located in the eastern half of the country. However, on the whole, hillforts are more numerous in the southern half of Ireland, an area where the La Tène decorated material is almost entirely lacking, thus supporting the possibility of a duality of population or culture during the Iron Age.

The second category of hillfort tends to be more westerly and southwesterly in its distribution. It is characterized by the presence of two or more widely spaced ramparts. One fine example is the fort at Mooghaun North, in Co. Clare, close to where the 'great Clare find' of Late Bronze Age gold objects was discovered in 1854. The outermost of its imposing stone walls covers an area of about 18 hectares (45 acres), while that at Ballylin, Co. Limerick – perhaps the largest of all – is over 20 hectares (50 acres) in extent. A further example, known as the Grianán of Aileach, in Co. Donegal, has a large stone-built wall inside a number of earthen banks. Its internal wall-chambers have been linked by Richard Warner to Scottish duns, and it is quite possible that the stone fort, and others further down along the west coast of Ireland as far as Staigue Fort in Co. Kerry, may also be linked with Scotland, though their prehistoric dating is open to considerable question. Dún Aenghus on the Aran Islands, a hillfort of the second category, ought possibly to be associated with stone forts such as the Grianán of Aileach. A fibula of around the first century BC was found within its walls by some boys hunting rabbits in the last century, but this is insufficient evidence for attaching the same date to the walls. The addition of *chevaux-de-frise*, mentioned earlier in this chapter, raises the question of connections for these stone forts with the Iberian Peninsula, but the link is at best unproven, and perhaps even non-existent.

A third category consists of two inland promontory forts in Co. Antrim – Luriegethan and Knockdhu, which could possibly have been built by invaders coming up the Irish Sea from Britain or Brittany, where the Veneti had multi-vallate promontory forts. A much smaller inland promontory fort is Caherconree in Co. Kerry, situated at a height of over 610 m. As it is unlikely to have been occupied on a permanent basis at such an altitude, it raises the whole question of the purpose or purposes of hillforts at much lower altitudes, where they vary from 0.4 to 20 hectares

133, 134

135

133 The fortifications at Dún Aenghus, Inishmore, Co. Galway, with defensive *chevaux-de-frise* in the foreground. See also ill. 134.

(1–50 acres) in size. Were they permanently occupied, or built as temporary refuges in time of danger – or could they have been centres for local gatherings such as annual fairs? Until more examples are excavated, it is as difficult to answer these questions as it is to provide satisfactory datings for each individual example.

The explanation as places of tribal assembly and possibly also for ceremonial purposes is more likely for a small number of sites where the ditch is unexpectedly inside the bank, making use as a defence unlikely. Examples at Navan Fort and Dún Ailinne have already been noted, but another most important example is Ráth na Ríogh – the Fort of the Kings – at Tara in Co. Meath. Here the bank enclosed a hill-top which, although only 152 m high, commands an impressive view in all directions. Inside the interior ditch there was a further trench, probably erected after the bank for defensive purposes. But, as at Navan Fort, it has not yet proved possible to relate the date of the bank to any of the structures which it encloses. These include two conjoined ringforts, in one of which now stands the *Lia Fáil*, the Stone of Destiny, the most obviously phallic symbol of ancient Ireland, and a monument which stresses the ritual importance of the site. That the sanctity of the site goes far back beyond the Iron Age is shown by a mound which also stood within Rath na Ríogh, namely the Mound of the Hostages which, on excavation, proved to be a

105, 106

136

134 (*Overleaf*) Aerial view of Dún Aenghus fort. The *chevaux-de-frise* appear as a rough, darker area in a wide band around the outer wall.

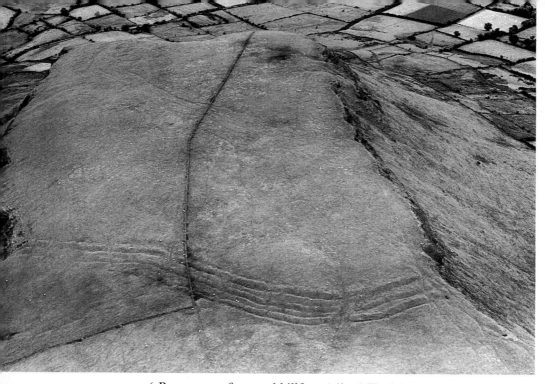

135,136 **Promontory forts and hillforts** (*Above*) The inland promontory fort at Luriegethan Co. Antrim. (*Below*) Aerial view of the Hill of Tara, Co. Meath, with (from left to right) the circular Rath of the Synods, the passage-tomb known as the Mound of the Hostages, and at right two conjoined ring-forts.

passage-tomb of *c*.2130 bc. Aligned to the Mound of the Hostages is the so-called 'Banqueting Hall', which gets its (modern) name because it has been wrongly identified with a structure mentioned as having been on Tara in medieval literary sources, and while this long-sunken rectangular area is most likely to be Neolithic in date, it is possible that it could have been the ceremonial entrance to the Hill on which all the major roads of ancient Ireland converged.

Between these two monuments – the Mound of the Hostages and the 'Banqueting Hall' – is a multi-vallate fort known as the Rath of the Synods. In 1899 it was 'excavated' by the British Israelites who were   136 searching for the biblical Ark of the Covenant which they believed had been brought there by the daughters of Zedekiah, one of whom was named Tea – whom they must have wanted to see as the person after whom the site (*Teamhair* in Irish) was named. Among the few finds which they are known to have made were a group of third century AD Roman coins which had been hidden in their excavation path a few days earlier so that they would not be disappointed! But when the site was re-excavated by Seán P. Ó Ríordáin in the early 1950s, it did by a curious coincidence produce genuine Roman material – a seal, a lock, glass and pottery, dating from the first to the third centuries AD. Concentric ditches and post-holes for wooden structures were also unearthed. While the excavations have sadly not yet been published, Caulfield has hinted that the rath may be later than the Roman finds. Raths, or ringforts, elsewhere have been claimed to belong to the Iron Age, but as yet there is no clear evidence to show that raths were built before the arrival of Christianity.

There are remains of many other earthworks on the Hill of Tara, including some circles and mounds visible in Leo Swan's aerial   136 photograph. Even if we cannot interpret them all, or identify them with structures named in medieval descriptions, these monuments, when taken together, show the Hill of Tara to have been an enigmatic multi-period site, but one which was certainly of major importance, as the historical records testify. Tara was the seat of the High Kingship of Ireland, even though few if any of those who reigned there ever extended their dominion over the whole of Ireland. In the dim shadows where mythology and history converge, Tara seems to have been in the hands of a Leinster dynasty, the Laigin. But in the early records, one can glimpse at their defeat at the hands of the Uí Néill, a dynasty which was to play an extremely important role in the first 500 years of christianized Ireland. The latter's origins were not local, however, for there is more than a hint that they were connected with the Connachta, a people descended from a legendary hero, Conn of the Hundred Battles, but also one which gives its name to Ireland's western province of Connacht.

The centre of Connachta power was Cruachan, a most puzzling complex of monuments on the plains of Roscommon. Apart from Uisneach in Co. Westmeath, it was the other most important royal and ceremonial site in Ireland after Navan Fort, Tara and Dún Ailinne, though it was also the location of one of the great fairs of ancient Ireland, with its teeming multitudes playing games and riding horses. Its traditional importance in the cult of ancestors is seen in the fact that it was also regarded as one of Ireland's most important cemeteries – and one of its entrances to the Underworld.

The site itself stretches over about 4 square miles, and comprises a considerable variety of monuments, including a number of circular earthworks as well as mounds, which may form a part of the cemetery of the old tales. The central monument is Rathcroghan mound with a broad flattened top, but excavations alone can show whether this was for habitation or a burial mound, perhaps even cognate to the Mound of the Hostages at Tara. Only minor excavations have taken place at Rathcroghan, but the whole area would suggest that there are monuments of various periods here, stretching from megalithic tombs to Bronze Age cairns and even as far as forts of the Christian period. The literary evidence suggests that the royal site may have been abandoned by about AD 800, so that there is a considerable possibility that some of the circular earthen structures may have been in use before St Patrick's time in the fifth century AD.

However, most of the early references to Cruachan, or Rathcroghan, belong more to the literary than to the historical sphere, so such speculation may not be entirely valid. What does emerge from those references is that Cruachan was the seat of Ailill (pron. Alil), king of the Connachtmen, and his wife Medhbh (pron. Maeve), an Irish Boadicea, whose name 'the drunken' is also associated with the goddess of sovereignty at Tara. Indeed, it is thought likely that the Uí Néill who ousted the Laigin from Tara came from Connacht, and were connected with the family which ruled at Cruachan. It is of significance, therefore, that in the focal Irish tale of *The Cattle Raid of Cooley*, Medhbh allies herself with men from Leinster to proceed against Connacht's traditional rivals, the Ulstermen, led by King Connor at Navan Fort, and championed by Cú Chulainn. Historically, it would appear that the armies of Connacht invaded Ulster in the fourth or fifth century, possibly in two waves, first under the Collas, two brothers, and later under the Uí Néill, who sent the local Ulaid tribe packing eastwards from Navan Fort, and then took over this part of Armagh for themselves.

There are considerable remains of linear earthworks – elongated tall banks – which stretch, with large interruptions, from Co. Sligo to Co. Monaghan, and which bear various names such as 'The Black Pig's Dyke', 'Dane's Cast' and 'Worm Ditch'. These have been considered to be part of a kind of 'Maginot Line' erected to defend Ulster against marauding Connachtmen from the south, like those portrayed in the *Cattle Raid of Cooley*. But the dating of these earthworks is unknown. However, another interesting earthwork, known as 'The Dorsey', in Co.

137 Two stone-carved animals, probably of Iron Age date, in the Church of Ireland Cathedral in Armagh.

Armagh, about 10 miles west-southwest of Newry, has recently been shown by dendrochronological means to have been built at the same time as the wooden circles at Navan Fort, around 100 BC. This means that 'The Dorsey' – and perhaps some of the other linear earthworks – are not only earlier than Hadrian's or the Antonine Wall in northern Britain, on which some considered them to have been modelled, but are also earlier than the historically known Connacht invasions of Ulster in the fourth or fifth century. If they were defences – and this is by no means proven – it would suggest that the fourth century thrust into Ulster from the south was not the first of its kind. But the contemporaneity of 'The Dorsey' and Navan Fort makes it probable that they were both erected by the lords of Navan Fort.

It has been widely accepted that the settlement on Cathedral Hill, Armagh, came into being when St Patrick founded a bishopric there in AD 444. But excavations on the site have revealed an earlier occupation of the hill, in the form of a ditch surrounding the hill-top which provided a radiocarbon date of c.AD 290. This, however, still leaves open the possibility that Cathedral Hill, in the centre of the modern city of Armagh, may have been the successor to Navan Fort.

On this hill there are a certain number of interesting stone sculptures which may well date from the period of prehistoric occupation of the site. Among these are attractive animal sculptures, and also a stone figure    137 known as the Tanderagee Idol, which may be wearing a horned helmet. It may, thus, represent some pagan deity. Other sculptures from the same province may also be prehistoric, most notable of which are the two now on Boa Island in Lower Lough Erne. One of these depicts two figures back to back, possibly modelled on the Roman Janus figures.

Such stone figures may have been the kind of Celtic pagan idols which were ousted by St Patrick, with whose arrival this book ends, though it may be said he was probably not the first Christian to have come to Ireland. But with him a new era dawned, which is dealt with in Máire and Liam de Paor's volume *Early Christian Ireland*. With this new era, the old pagan sites became deserted, and new Christian ones founded. Armagh may have taken over from Navan Fort before the arrival of St Patrick, but the transition can be seen at another of the royal sites already mentioned – 106 Dún Ailinne, which was abandoned in favour of the Christian site on a neighbouring hill. This departure from the old pagan sites, and the rising popularity of the new, was neatly summarized by the ascetic Aenghus who, writing in his Calendar around AD 800, said:

> Tara's mighty burgh perished at the death of her princes; with a multitude of venerable champions, the great height of Machae [Armagh] abides.
>
> Rathcroghan, it has vanished with Ailill, offspring of victory; fair the sovranty over princes that there is in the monastery of Clonmacnois.
>
> Ailenn's proud burgh has perished with its warlike host; great is victorious Brigit, fair is her multitudinous cemetery.
>
> Emhain's [Navan Fort's] burgh it hath vanished, save that the stones remain; the cemetery of the west of the world is multitudinous Glendalough.

# Epilogue

ON READING THESE PAGES, you might be forgiven for thinking that they are only about things and places . . . and not about people, human beings who lived and thought as we do, and who were hatched, matched and dispatched as man and woman have been since the days of Adam and Eve. And you might be right – at least up to a point. For those who lived in an age before writing have the disadvantage that their story can only be told from the mute testimonies which they themselves left behind. It is obviously, therefore, a very incomplete story. The monuments and objects which do survive are only a skeleton to try to build some flesh on, a framework for interpretation. Through these, we begin to get within reach of prehistoric people.

It is only through a great monument like Newgrange that we feel we can begin to come to grips with the higher thought processes and religion of our ancient ancestors, though we cannot say how many people were involved in building this monument, or what, indeed, the population numbers in Ireland were like at any given time. However, the more mundane, mechanical things – the axes, the houses, the graves – do give us an insight into the everyday life, death and burial of those in prehistory. In many respects, the basic style of life in prehistoric Ireland was not too far different from the folk-life we know to have survived down to the last century, and even into this. For Ireland, on the geographical periphery of the Eurasian landmass, is a country which moves at a slightly slower pace than others, and thereby preserves some old and respected traditions which have sadly died out elsewhere. That, in itself, is no disadvantage, and perhaps an added reason why the prehistory of Ireland is worth studying.

# Select Bibliography

This short bibliography is designed to provide the reader with a selection of the more significant recent publications, as well as some of the older standard works, which are relevant to the contents of this volume. While not covering every site mentioned or author quoted in the text, the books and articles listed here provide bibliographies which will usually refer the reader to other important literature not cited below. Note that where Colloquia, Festschriften and similar volumes contain a number of articles pertinent to the subject matter of this book, these articles are not listed separately, and the reader is recommended to consult each of them, where possible, to ensure proper coverage for any one period. The works listed as 'General' should also be consulted for each period. Useful summaries of excavations may be found in the Association of Young Irish Archaeologists' *Excavations* volumes of the period 1970-76 (ed. T. Delaney) and 1985 (ed. C. Cotter), and to keep in touch with current research, the reader would be well advised to consult the *British Archaeological Bibliography*, published twice yearly and available by subscription from the Council for British Archaeology, Bowes Morrell House, 111 Walmgate, York, YO1 2UA.

The following abbreviations are used in the bibliography below:

| | |
|---|---|
| *BAR* | British Archaeological Reports |
| *JCHAS* | Journal of the Cork Historical and Archaeological Society |
| *JRSAI* | Journal of the Royal Society of Antiquaries of Ireland |
| *PPS* | Proceedings of the Prehistoric Society |
| *PRIA* | Proceedings of the Royal Irish Academy |
| *UJA* | Ulster Journal of Archaeology |

## General

BAILLIE, M.G.L., 'Irish Dendrochronology and Radiocarbon Calibration', *UJA* 48 (1985): 11–23

DE LAET, S.J. (ed.), *Acculturation and Continuity in Atlantic Europe mainly during the Neolithic Period and the Bronze Age*, Fourth Atlantic Colloquium, Dissertationes Archaeologicae Gandenses XVI, Bruges 1976.

EDWARDS, K.J. and WARREN, W.P. (eds.), *The Quaternary History of Ireland*, London 1985.

EVANS, E., *Prehistoric and Early Christian Ireland. A Guide*, London 1966.

–, *The Personality of Ireland*, 2nd ed., Belfast 1981.

HAMLIN, A., *Historic Monuments of Northern Ireland*, Belfast 1983.

HARBISON, P., *Guide to the National and Historic Monuments of Ireland*, Dublin 1993

HERITY, M. and EOGAN, G., *Ireland in Prehistory*, London 1977.

LYNCH, A., 'Man and Environment in South-West Ireland 4000 BC–800 AD', *BAR*, British Series 85, Oxford 1981.

MALLORY, J.P. and McNEILL, T.E., *The Archaeology of Ulster*, Belfast 1991.

MITCHELL, F., *The Shell Guide to Reading the Irish Landscape*, Dublin 1986.

NORMAN, E.R. and ST JOSEPH, J.K.S., *The Early Development of Irish Society, The Evidence of Aerial Photography*, Cambridge 1969.

Ó CORRÁIN, D. (ed.), *Irish Antiquity, Essays and Studies presented to Professor M.J. O'Kelly*, Cork 1981.

Ó RIORDÁIN, S.P., *Antiquities of the Irish Countryside*, 5th ed., London 1979.

RYAN, M. (ed.), *The Origin of Metallurgy in Atlantic Europe*, Fifth Atlantic Colloquium, Dublin 1979.

–, *Treasures of Ireland, Irish Art 3000 BC–1500 AD*, Dublin 1983.

SCOTT, B.G., (ed.), *Studies on Early Ireland, Essays in Honour of M.V. Duignan*, Belfast 1981.

WADDELL, J., 'The Invasion Hypothesis in Irish Prehistory', *Antiquity* 52 (1978): 121–28.

## Chapter 2 The Search for the First Settlers

MITCHELL, G.F. and SIEVEKING, G. DE G., 'Flint Flake, Probably of Palaeolithic Age, from Mell Townland, near Drogheda, Co. Louth, Ireland', *JRSAI* 102 (1972): 174–77.

RYAN, M., 'Archaeological Excavations at Lough Boora, Boughal Townland, Co. Offaly', in J. Cooke (ed.), *Proceedings of the Seventh International Peat Congress*, Dublin 1984, Vol. I, 407–12.

WOODMAN, P.C., 'Recent Excavations at Newferry, Co. Antrim', *PPS* 43 (1977): 155–99.

–, 'The Mesolithic in Ireland', *BAR*, British Series 58, Oxford 1978.

–, 'The Early Prehistory of Munster', *JCHAS* 89 (1984): 1–11.

–, *Excavations at Mount Sandel 1973–77*, Belfast 1985.

## Chapter 3 Farmers and Megalith-builders

APSIMON, A.M., 'An Early Neolithic House in Co. Tyrone', *JRSAI* 99 (1969): 165–68.

BRINDLEY, A. L. and LANTING, J. N., 'Radiocarbon Dates for Neolithic Single Burials', *Journal of Irish Archaeology* V (1989/90): 1–7.

–, 'Radiocarbon Dates from the Cemetery at Poulawack, Co. Clare', *Journal of Irish Archaeology* VI (1991/92): 13–17.

BURENHULT, G., *The Archaeology of Carrowmore*, Theses and Papers in North-European Archaeology 14, Stockholm 1984.

CAPONIGRO, P., *Megaliths*, New York 1986.

CASE, H., 'Irish Neolithic Pottery: Distribution and Sequence', *PPS* 27 (1961): 174–233.

–, 'Neolithic Explanations', *Antiquity* 43 (1969): 176–86.

–, 'Settlement-patterns in the North Irish Neolithic', *UJA* 32 (1969): 3–27.

–, 'A Ritual Site in North-East Ireland', in G. Daniel and P. Kjaerum (eds.), *Megalithic Graves and Ritual*, Third Atlantic Colloquium, Jutland Archaeological Society Publications XI (1973): 173–96.

CAULFIELD, S., 'Neolithic Fields: the Irish Evidence', in H.C. Bowen and P.J. Fowler (eds.), *Early Land Allotment in the British Isles, BAR*, British Series 48, Oxford 1978, 137–43.

COONEY, G., 'Some Aspects of the Siting of Megalithic Tombs in County Leitrim', *JRSAI* 109 (1979): 74–91.

DANIEL, G., 'Megalithic Studies in Ireland, 1929–79', *UJA* 43 (1980): 1–8.

DARVILL, T.C., 'Court Cairns, Passage Graves and Social Change in Ireland', *Man* 14 (1979): 311–27.

DE VALERA, R., 'The Court Cairns of Ireland', *PRIA* 60 C (1960): 9–140.

–, and Ó NUALLÁIN, S., *Survey of the Megalithic Tombs of Ireland*, Dublin, Vol. I – Co. Clare, 1961; Vol. II – Co. Mayo, 1964; Vol. III – Counties Galway, Roscommon, Leitrim, Longford, Westmeath, Laoighis, Offaly, Kildare and Cavan, 1972; Vol. V – Co. Sligo, 1989.

EOGAN, G., *Excavations at Knowth 1*, Dublin 1984.

–, *Knowth and the Passage-Tombs of Ireland*, London 1986.

EVANS, E.E., *Lyles Hill: A Late Neolithic Site in County Antrim*, Belfast 1953.

GOWEN, M., 'Tankardstown, Co. Limerick: A Neolithic House', *Archaeology Ireland* 1 (1) (1987): 6–10.

–, 'A Neolithic House at Newtown', *Archaeology Ireland* 6 (2) (1992): 25–27.

HERITY, M., *Irish Passage Graves*, Dublin 1974.

–, 'Irish Decorated Neolithic Pottery', *PRIA* 82 C (1982): 247–404.

–, 'The Finds from Irish Court Tombs', *PRIA* 87 C (1987): 103–281.

JOPE, E.M., 'Porcellanite Axes from Factories in North-East Ireland: Tievebulliagh and Rathlin', *UJA* 15 (1952): 31–55.

KITCHIN, F.T., 'The Carrowmore Megalithic Cemetery, Co. Sligo', *PPS* 49 (1983): 151–75.

MALLORY, J.P. and HARTWELL, B., 'Donegore', *Current Archaeology* 8 (1984): 271–75.

MANNING, C., 'A Neolithic Burial Mound at Ashleypark, Co. Tipperary', *PRIA* 85 C (1985): 61–100.

O'KELLY, C., 'Passage-grave Art in the Boyne Valley', *PPS* 39 (1973): 354–82.

O'KELLY, M.J., 'Some Thoughts on the Megalithic Tombs of Ireland', in Megaw, J.V.S. (ed.), *To Illustrate the Monuments: Essays on Archaeology Presented to Stuart Piggott*, London 1976, 126–33.

–, *Newgrange*, London and New York 1982.

–, 'The Megalithic Tombs of Ireland', in C. Renfrew (ed.), *The Megalithic Monuments of Western Europe*, London 1983, 113–26.

Ó NUALLÁIN, S., 'A Neolithic House at Ballyglass, near Ballycastle, Co. Mayo', *JRSAI* 102 (1972): 49–57.

–, 'The Megalithic Tombs of Ireland', *Expedition* (Pennsylvania) 21, No. 3 (1979): 5–15.

–, 'Irish Portal Tombs: Topography, Siting and Distribution', *JRSAI* 113 (1983): 75–105.

Ó RÍORDÁIN, S.P., 'Lough Gur Excavations: Neolithic and Bronze Age Houses on Knockadoon', *PRIA* 56 C (1954): 297–459.

RENFREW C., 'The Social Archaeology of Megalithic Monuments', *Scientific American* 249, No.5 (1983): 128–36.

ROCHE, H., 'Pre-Tomb Habitation found at Knowth, Co. Meath, Spring 1989', *Archaeology Ireland* 3 (3) (1989): 101–03.

SHEE TWOHIG, E., *The Megalithic Art of Western Europe*, Oxford 1981.

–, *Irish Megalithic Tombs*, Princes Risborough 1990.

WATERMAN, D.M., 'The Excavation of a Court Cairn at Tully, County Fermanagh', *UJA* 41 (1978): 3–14

## Chapter 4 The Rise of Metalworking

APSIMON, A., 'The Earlier Bronze Age in the North of Ireland', *UJA* 32 (1969): 28–72.

BRINDLEY, A., 'The Cinerary Urn Tradition in Ireland – An Alternative Interpretation', *PRIA* 80 C (1980): 197–206

BRINDLEY, A.L., LANTING, J.N., and MOOK, W.G., 'Radiocarbon Dates from Moneen and Labbacallee, County Cork', *Journal of Irish Archaeology* IV (1987/88): 13–20.

–, 'Radiocarbon Dates from Irish Fulachta Fiadh and other Burnt Mounds', *Journal of Irish Archaeology* V (1989/90): 25–33.

BRINDLEY, A.L. and LANTING, J.N., 'Radiocarbon Dates from Wedge Tombs', *Journal of Irish Archaeology* VI (1991/92): 19–26.

BUCKLEY, V. (ed.), *Burnt Offerings*, Dublin 1990.

BURGESS, C., *The Age of Stonehenge*, London 1980.

BURL, A., *The Stone Circles of The British Isles*, New Haven/London 1976.

CASE, H., 'The Beaker Culture in Britain and Ireland', in Mercer R. (ed.), *Beakers in Britain and Europe: Four Studies, BAR* Supplementary Series 26, Oxford 1977, 71–101.

CLAYTON, B., 'Metal Analyses – Their Limitation

and Application to the Early Bronze Age in Ireland', *Bulletin of the Institute of Archaeology of the University of London* 11 (1974): 75–129.

COGHLAN, H.H. and RAFTERY, J. 'Irish Prehistoric Casting Moulds', *Sibrium* 6 (1961): 223–44.

COLLINS, A.E.P., 'Bronze Age Moulds in Ulster', *UJA* 33 (1970): 23–36.

DE VALERA, R. and O NUALLÁIN, S., *Survey of the Megalithic Tombs of Ireland*, Vol. IV – Counties Cork, Kerry, Limerick and Tipperary, Dublin 1982.

EOGAN, G., 'Some Observations on the Middle Bronze Age in Ireland', *JRSAI* 92 (1962): 45–60.

FLANAGAN, L.N.W., 'The Composition of Irish Bronze Age Cemeteries', *Irish Archaeological Research Forum* III, 2 (1976): 7–20.

–, 'The Irish Earlier Bronze Age Industry in Perspective', *JRSAI* 112 (1982): 93–100.

GROENMAN-VAN WAATERINGE, W., and BUTLER, J.J., 'The Ballynoe Stone Circle. Excavations by A.E. Van Giffen 1937–1938', *Palaeohistoria* 18 (1976): 73–104.

HADINGHAM, E., *Ancient Carvings in Britain: A Mystery*, London 1974.

HARBISON, P., *The Axes of the Early Bronze Age in Ireland*, Prähistorische Bronzefunde IX, 1, Munich 1969.

–, *The Daggers and the Halberds of the Early Bronze Age in Ireland*, Prähistorische Bronzefunde VI, 1, Munich 1969.

–, 'The Earlier Bronze Age in Ireland', *JRSAI* 103 (1973): 93–152.

HARTWELL, B., 'Ballynahatty: A Prehistoric Ceremonial Centre', *Archaeology Ireland* 5 (4) (1991): 12–15.

HAWKES, C., 'Gold Ear-rings of the Bronze Age, East and West', *Folklore* 72 (1961): 438–74.

JACKSON, J.S., 'Bronze Age Copper Mining in Counties Cork and Kerry, Ireland', in P.T. Craddock (ed.), *Scientific Studies in Early Mining and Extractive Metallurgy*, British Musuem Occasional Paper 20, London 1980, 9–30.

–, 'Copper Mining at Mount Gabriel, Co. Cork: Bronze Age Bonanza or Post-famine Fiasco? A reply', *PPS* 50 (1984): 375–77.

KAVANAGH, R., 'The Encrusted Urn in Ireland', *PRIA* 73 C (1973): 507–617.

–, 'Collared and Cordoned Cinerary Urns in Ireland', *PRIA* 76 C (1976): 293–403.

LUCAS, A.T., 'Toghers or Causeways: Some Evidence from Archaeological, Literary, Historical and Place-name Sources', *PRIA* 85 C (1985): 37–60.

MACWHITE, E., 'A New View on Irish Bronze Age Rock-scribings', *JRSAI* 76 (1946): 59–80.

O'KELLY, M.J., 'Excavation of a Cairn at Moneen, Co. Cork', *PRIA* 54 C (1952): 121–59.

–, 'Excavations and Experiments in Ancient Irish Cooking-places', *JRSAI* 84 (1954): 105–55.

–, 'An Axe Mould from Lyre, Co. Cork', *JCHAS* 75 (1970): 25–28.

–, CLEARY, R.M. and LEHANE, D., 'Newgrange,

Co. Meath, Ireland. The Late Neolithic-Beaker Period Settlement', *BAR*, International Series 190, Oxford 1983.

Ó NUALLÁIN, S., 'A Survey of Stone Circles in Cork and Kerry', *PRIA* 84 C (1984): 1–77.

PATRICK, J. and FREEMAN, P.R., 'Revised Surveys of Cork-Kerry Stone Circles', *Archaeoastronomy* 5 (*Journal of the History of Astronomy* 14), 1983, S50–56.

POLLOCK, A. and WATERMAN, D.M., 'A Bronze Age Habitation Site at Downpatrick', *UJA* 27 (1964): 31–58.

RAFTERY, J., 'The Tumulus-Cemetery of Carrowjames, Co. Mayo', *Journal of the Galway Archaeological and Historical Society* 18 (1938): 157–67 and 19 (1940): 16–88.

SHERIDAN, A., 'A Reconsideration of the Origins of Irish Metallurgy', *The Journal of Irish Archaeology* I (1983): 11–19.

SWEETMAN, P.D., 'An Earthen Enclosure at Monknewtown, Slane, Co. Meath', *PRIA* 76 C (1976): 25–72.

–, 'A Late Neolithic/Early Bronze Age Pit Circle at Newgrange, Co. Meath', *PRIA* 85 C (1985): 195–221.

TAYLOR, J.J., *Bronze Age Goldwork of the British Isles*, Cambridge 1980.

THOM, A.S., 'The Stone Rings of Beaghmore: Geometry and Astronomy', *UJA* 43 (1980): 15–19.

WADDELL, J., 'Irish Bronze Age Cists: A Survey', *JRSAI* 100 (1970): 91–139.

–, 'The Encrusted Urn in Ireland: Some Comments', *Irish Archaeological Research Forum* 2, No.1 (1975): 21–28.

–, 'Knocknagur, Turoe and Local Enquiry', *Journal of the Galway Archaeological and Historical Society* 40, 1985/86, 130–33.

–, *The Bronze Age Burials of Ireland*, Galway 1990.

WIJNGAARDEN-BAKKER, L.H. van, 'The Animal Remains from the Beaker Settlement at Newgrange, Co. Meath: Final Report', *PRIA* 86 C (1986): 2–111.

WOODMAN, P.C., 'Filling in the Spaces in Irish Prehistory', *Antiquity* 66 (1992): 295–314.

## Chapter 5 A Golden Age

BARRY, T.B., 'Archaeological excavations at Dunbeg Promontory Fort, Co. Kerry, 1977', *PRIA* 81 C (1981): 295–329.

CHAMPION, T., 'The End of the Irish Bronze Age', *North Munster Antiquarian Journal* 14 (1971): 17–24.

COLES, J.M., 'European Bronze Age Shields', *PPS* 28 (1962): 156–90.

–, 'Irish Bronze Age Horns and Their Relations with Northern Europe', *PPS* 29 (1963): 326–56.

EOGAN, G., 'The Later Bronze Age in Ireland in the Light of Recent Research', *PPS* 30 (1964): 268–351.

–, 'Regionale Gruppierungen in der Spätbronzezeit Irlands', *Archäologisches Korrespondenzblatt* 4 (1974): 319–27.

–, *The Hoards of the Irish Later Bronze Age*, Dublin 1983.

HAWKES, C.F.C. and CLARKE, R.R., 'Gahlstorf and Caister-on-Sea: Two Finds of Late Bronze Age Irish Gold', in I. Ll. Foster and L. Alcock (eds.), *Culture and Environment, Essays in Honour of Sir Cyril Fox*, London 1963, 193–250.

HAWKES, C.F.C. and SMITH, M.A., 'On Some Buckets and Cauldrons of the Bronze and Early Iron Ages', *The Antiquaries Journal* 37 (1957): 131–98.

LYNN, C.J., 'The Excavation of a Ring-cairn in Carnkenny Townland, Co. Tyrone', *UJA* 36/37 (1973–74): 17–31.

HENCKEN, H. O'N., 'Ballinderry Crannog No. 2', *PRIA* 47 C (1942): 1–76.

RAFTERY, B., 'Rathgall: A Late Bronze Age Burial in Ireland', *Antiquity* 47 (1973): 293–95.

–, 'Rathgall and Irish Hillfort Problems', in D.W. Harding (ed.), *Hillforts, Later Prehistoric Earthworks in Britain and Ireland*, London 1976, 339–57, 478–82 and 532–39.

–, 'Two Recently Discovered Bronze Shields from the Shannon Basin', *JRSAI* 112 (1982): 5–17.

RAFTERY, J., 'The Gorteenreagh Hoard', in E. Rynne (ed.), *North Munster Studies, Essays in Commemoration of Monsignor Michael Moloney*, Limerick 1967, 61–71.

POWELL, T.G.E., 'The Sintra Collar and the Shannongrove Gorget: Aspects of Late Bronze Age Goldwork in the West of Europe', *North Munster Antiquarian Journal* 16 (1973–74): 3–13.

## Chapter 6 The Celtic Iron Age

BROWN, C.G. and HARPER, A.E.T., 'Excavations on Cathedral Hill, Armagh, 1968', *UJA* 47 (1984): 109–61.

'COLLOQUIUM on Hiberno-Roman Relations and Material Remains', *PRIA* 76 C (1976): 171–292.

COPLESTONE-CROW, B., 'The Dual Nature of the Irish Colonization of Dyfed in the Dark Ages', *Studia Celtica* 16–17 (1981–82): 1–24.

COTTER, C., 'Atlantic Fortifications: the Duns of the Aran Islands', *Archaeology Ireland* 8 (1) (1994): 24–28.

DILLON, M., 'The Irish Settlements in Wales', *Celtica* 12 (1977): 1–11.

DUIGNAN, M., 'The Turoe Stone: Its Place in Insular La Tène Art', in P.M. Duval and C. Hawkes (eds.), *Celtic Art in Ancient Europe, Five Protohistoric Centuries*, London 1976, 201–17.

EMANIA, Bulletin of the Navan Research Group 1–10, 1986–92.

HAMLIN, A., 'Emain Macha: Navan Fort', *Seanchas Ardmhacha* 11, No. 2 (1985): 295–300.

HARBISON, P., 'Wooden and Stone *Chevaux-de-frise* in Central and Western Europe', *PPS* 37 (1971): 195–225.

HERITY, M., 'A Survey of the Royal Site of Cruachain in Connacht', *JRSAI* 113 (1983): 121–42 and 114 (1984) 125–38.

IRELAND, A., 'The Finding of the "Clonmacnoise" Gold Torcs', *PRIA* 92 C (1992): 123–46.

LUCAS, A.T., 'Prehistoric Block-wheels from Doogarymore, Co. Roscommon, and Timahoe East, Co. Kildare', *JRSAI* 102 (1972): 19–48.

MACEOIN, G. (ed.), *Proceedings of the Sixth International Congress of Celtic Studies*, Dublin 1983.

MALLORY, J.P., 'The Origins of the Irish', The Journal of Irish Archaeology II (1984): 65–69.

–, *Navan Fort, The Ancient Capital of Ulster*, Belfast 1985.

O'KELLY, M.J., 'The Cork Horns, the Petrie Crown and the Bann Disc', *JCHAS* 66 (1961): 1–12.

RAFTERY, B., *A Catalogue of Irish Iron Age Antiquities*, 2 Vols., Marburg 1983.

–, *La Tène in Ireland: Problems of Origin and Chronology*, Marburg 1984.

–, 'A Wooden Trackway of Iron Age Date in Ireland', *Antiquity* 60 (1986): 50–53.

–, *Trackways through Time*, Rush 1990.

–, *Pagan Celtic Ireland: The Enigma of the Irish Iron Age*, London and New York 1994.

SCOTT, B.G., 'The Origins and Early Development of Iron Use in Ireland', in H. Haefner (ed.), *Frühes Eisen in Europa, Festschrift Guyan*, Schaffhausen 1981, 101–8.

SWAN, D.L., 'The Hill of Tara, County Meath: The Evidence of Aerial Photography', *JRSAI* 108 (1978): 51–66.

THOMAS, C. (ed.), *The Iron Age in the Irish Sea Province*, Council for British Archaeology, Research Report 9, London 1972.

WADDELL, J., 'Rathcroghan – A Royal Site in Connacht', *The Journal of Irish Archaeology* I (1983): 21–46.

WAILES, B., 'Dún Ailinne: An Interim Report', in D.W. Harding (ed.), *Hillforts, Later Prehistoric Earthworks in Britain and Ireland*, London 1976, 319–38, 474–77 and 531.

–, 'The Irish "Royal Sites" in History and Archaeology', *Cambridge Medieval Celtic Studies* 3 (1982): 1–29.

WARNER, R.B., 'Ireland, Ulster and Scotland in the Earlier Iron Age', in A. O'Connor and D.V. Clark (eds.), *From the Stone Age to the 'Forty-five, Studies Presented to R.B.K. Stevenson*, Edinburgh 1983, 160–87.

# List of Illustrations

Unless otherwise credited, drawings are by Edelgard Soergel-Harbison. Photo credits are abbreviated as follows: BM (Trustees of the British Museum), CUCAP (Cambridge University Collection of Air Photographs), PC (Paul Caponigro), CPWI (Commissioners of Public Works in Ireland), PH (Peter Harbison), ITB (Irish Tourist Board), NMI (National Museum of Ireland) and DLS (D.L.Swan). The Paul Caponigro photographs are reproduced from *Megaliths* by Paul Caponigro, © 1986, by permission of Little, Brown and Co., in association with the New York Graphic Society.

*Half-title page* Newgrange spiral. Photo ITB.
*Title page* The 'Tanderagee Idol'. Photo PH.

1 Map of prehistoric Ireland. Drawn by Hanni Bailey.
2 Plaque commemorating Sir William Wilde in Dublin. Photo PH.
3 Palaeolithic flint from Mell, Co. Louth. After Sieveking and Mitchell.
4 Mesolithic house remains, Mount Sandel, Co. Derry. Photo Peter Woodman.
5 Microliths from Mount Sandel. After Woodman.
6 Flint tools from Mount Sandel. After Woodman.
7 Mounted projectile heads from Mount Sandel. After Woodman.
8 Stone axe from Lough Boora, Co. Offaly. After Ryan.
9 Neolithic house plan, Ballynagilly, Co. Tyrone. After ApSimon.
10 Distribution map of Neolithic axes. Drawn by Michael Gleeson after Jope and Rynne.
11 Air view of Ballyglass, Co. Mayo. Photo DLS.
12 Plan of fields at Behy/Glenulra, Co. Mayo. After Caulfield.
13 Lough Gur, Co. Limerick, c.1946. Photo ITB.
14 Two Neolithic houses at Lough Gur. After Ó Ríordáin.
15 Air view of Lyles Hill, Co. Antrim. Photo CUCAP, Crown copyright.
16 'Western Neolithic' pottery. After Case.
17 Decorated Neolithic pottery. After Herity.
18 'Carrowkeel' pot. Photo CPWI.
19 Distribution maps of the four types of megalithic tomb. Courtesy Irish Megalithic Survey.
20 Montage of excavation of Grave 27, Carrowmore, Co. Sligo. Photo G. Burenhult.
21 Walrus bone ring and antler pin from Grave 27, Carrowmore. Photo G. Burenhult.
22 Court cairn at Creevykeel, Co. Sligo. Photo CPWI.
23 Plans of court cairns: (top left) after Davies and Evans; (top right) after Kilbride-Jones; (below left) after Hencken; (below right) after De Valera.
24 Portal-tomb at Kilclooney, Co. Donegal. Photo PH.
25 Portal-tomb at Legananny, Co. Down. Photo PC.
26 View of Carrowmore, Grave 7. Photo ITB.
27 Bone pins from Fourknocks and Knowth, Co. Meath. After Hartnett and Eogan.
28 Passage-tombs E and F at Carrowkeel, Co. Sligo. After Macalister, Armstrong and Praeger.
29 Aerial view of the passage-tombs at Loughcrew, Co. Meath. Photo CUCAP.
30 Cairn S at Loughcrew. Photo PC.
31 Interior of Cairn T at Loughcrew, with decorated stone. Photo CPWI.
32 Selection of art motifs used on passage tombs in Co. Meath. After C. O'Kelly.
33 Map of monuments in the Boyne Valley, Co. Meath. Drawn by Michael Gleeson.
34 Section of main mound at Knowth, Co. Meath. Photo CPWI.
35 Aerial view of Knowth during excavations. Photo DLS.
36 Plan of the passage-tombs at Knowth. After Eogan.
37 Flint macehead from eastern tomb, Knowth. Photo CPWI.
38 Decoration on the macehead from Knowth. After Hilary Richardson's drawing from Eogan and Richardson.
39 Decorated stone basin in eastern tomb, Knowth. Photo CPWI.
40 Stone decorated with stylized human face, Knowth. Photo CPWI.
41 Entrance stone at Knowth. Photo PC.
42 Entrance stone at Newgrange. Photo ITB.
43 Kerbstone 52 at Newgrange. Photo CPWI.
44 Newgrange reconstructed. Photo CPWI.
45 Interior of tomb at Newgrange, looking towards entrance. Photo CPWI.
46 Roof of the chamber at Newgrange. Photo PC.

200

# Index